'In this book, you'll get pract
for making two game-changi... getting
out of your head, as well as taming your demons with warmth
rather than our habitual resistance, indulgence and denial.
The best part is that all of it is backed up by rigorous science'
Dan Harris, author of *10% Happier*

'Daniel Goleman and Tsoknyi Rinpoche teach
us how to look down the periscope of perception
and peer into our inner selves. They encourage
us to open up our lenses to see what's behind our
thoughts and emotions and wrap whatever we find
in compassion. This is the road to liberation.
They are the perfect guides for this journey'
Ruby Wax, author of *A Mindfulness
Guide for the Frazzled*

'This beautiful and inspiring book, arising
from the brilliance of two great minds, contains
profound yet practical advice on meditation
and its power to nourish the world'
Gelong Thubten, author of *A Monk's
Guide to Happiness*

'An exciting new book that combines recent
research into meditation with fresh, accessible
and profound teachings on the actual practice'
Pema Chödrön, author of *When Things Fall Apart*

'*Why We Meditate* is a rare blend of genuine,
far-reaching meditative wisdom and the cutting-edge
neuroscience that both explains and supports it.
This book is an extraordinary collaboration and a
great jewel that will benefit all who
read it. Highly recommended'
Joseph Goldstein, author of
Seeking the Heart of Wisdom

ABOUT THE AUTHORS

Daniel Goleman is the internationally bestselling author and co-author of several books, including *Emotional Intelligence*, *Focus*, and *The Science of Meditation*. He was a science reporter for the *New York Times*, was twice nominated for the Pulitzer Prize, and received the American Psychological Association's Lifetime Achievement Award for his writing. He lives in the Berkshires, USA. Find out more at DanielGoleman.info.

Tsoknyi Rinpoche is one of the most beloved teachers among the new generation of Tibetan Buddhist meditation masters. Widely recognized as an outstanding meditation teacher for more than twenty-five years, he is the author of *Open Heart, Open Mind*, *Fearless Simplicity*, and *Carefree Dignity*. He has received accolades from prominent Buddhist teachers, including His Holiness the Dalai Lama. Find out more at TsoknyiRinpoche.org.

WHY WE MEDITATE

ALSO BY DANIEL GOLEMAN

Vital Lies, Simple Truths
Emotional Intelligence
Working with Emotional Intelligence
Destructive Emotions
Social Intelligence
Primal Leadership (with Richard Boyatzis and Annie McKee)
Ecological Intelligence
Focus
A Force for Good
The Science of Meditation (with Richard Davidson)

ALSO BY TSOKNYI RINPOCHE

Carefree Dignity
Fearless Simplicity
Open Heart, Open Mind

WHY WE MEDITATE

7 Simple Practices
for a Calmer Mind

DANIEL GOLEMAN

AND

TSOKNYI RINPOCHE

WITH ADAM KANE

PENGUIN LIFE

AN IMPRINT OF

PENGUIN BOOKS

PENGUIN LIFE

UK | USA | Canada | Ireland | Australia
India | New Zealand | South Africa

Penguin Life is part of the Penguin Random House group of companies
whose addresses can be found at global.penguinrandomhouse.com.

Penguin
Random House
UK

First published in the United States of America by Atria Books,
an imprint of Simon & Schuster, Inc. 2022
First published in Great Britain by Penguin Life 2022
001

Interior design by Joy O'Meara @ Creative Joy Designs
Printed and bound in Great Britain by Clays Ltd, Elcograf S.p.A.

The authorized representative in the EEA is Penguin Random House Ireland,
Morrison Chambers, 32 Nassau Street, Dublin D02 YH68

A CIP catalogue record for this book is available from the British Library

ISBN: 978-0-241-52787-0

www.greenpenguin.co.uk

MIX
Paper from
responsible sources
FSC   FSC® C018179

Penguin Random House is committed to a
sustainable future for our business, our readers
and our planet. This book is made from Forest
Stewardship Council® certified paper.

For inner peace, a peaceful world, and the benefit of all beings

—— · ◆ · ——

CONTENTS

ONE

· — · ✦ · — ·

WHAT THIS BOOK OFFERS YOU

TSOKNYI RINPOCHE

I grew up in a village atmosphere, surrounded by a lot of love and care. I vividly remember as a small child repeatedly jumping onto and running off from the lap of my grandpa, who was wrapped in a *dagam*, a big, warm meditation cloak. My grandpa just kept meditating and murmuring mantras while freely letting the rascal come and go. My grandpa radiated warmth, love, and peace, no matter what was happening around him.

I was born in Kathmandu to Tulku Urgyen Rinpoche, a renowned Tibetan meditation master, and a Nepalese mother descended from a Tibetan family of meditators. My mother's ancestors numbered a famous king of Tibet whose descendants settled in Nubri, a Nepali valley in the shadow of Mount Manaslu, the eighth-highest mountain in the world. I spent my early childhood in that remote mountainous region.

Both sides of my family included dedicated and accomplished meditators, including my father, my father's grandmother, and her father, who was one of the legendary meditators of his time. Accomplishment in meditation generally means having passed through many stages of mind-training and becoming stable in wisdom and compassion. I was therefore privileged to be trained from childhood in meditation and nurtured in a meditative atmosphere.

At thirteen I was sent to a Tibetan refugee community in the Kangra Valley in northern India for formal Buddhist education. There I continued meditation training with several masters of the art, including yogis who practiced there in seclusion. And ever since, I've been fortunate in continuing to study with some of the foremost meditation masters of our times.

I started teaching Buddhism in my early twenties and have traveled the world since then, teaching meditation to tens of thousands of students on several continents. I have also continued to keep educating myself and to explore relevant scientific knowledge to the science of the mind. I attended several Mind & Life seminars where the Dalai Lama spoke with scientists, and I've taught meditation at the Mind & Life Summer Research Institute to graduate students and postdocs.

From the start of my meditation teaching my natural curiosity made me particularly interested in Western psychology, contemporary life, and the unique challenges modern people face. As a traveling teacher my lifestyle has meant ceaseless movement. Unlike many well-known Asian meditation teachers, I prefer to travel alone and anonymously, so I can observe and interact with people in spontaneous, authentic ways. I have spent a lot of time in airports, walking the streets of cities around the world, sitting in coffee shops, and, in general, people-watching.

I've spent decades with experts in psychology and science, and with friends and students around the world, trying to understand their mind-sets, struggles, and cultural pressures. I've gotten tutorials from several highly regarded psychotherapists, such as Tara Bennett-Goleman and John Welwood. With Tara (Daniel Goleman's wife), we explored many psychological themes, particularly common dysfunctional emotional patterns, such as feelings of emotional deprivation and fear of abandonment, which she has written about in her book *Emotional Alchemy* and elsewhere. John Welwood, a marital therapist and author, was a source of insight into relationship patterns as well as the concept of "spiritual bypassing," the tendency to use spiritual practices, such as meditation, to avoid unhealed psychological wounds and overwhelming, troubling emotions. I've also learned a tremendous amount from my students, from talking with them about their lives, their relationships, and their spiritual practice.

From these sources, I learned about both my own neuroses, habitual patterns, and emotions and those of my students. This has informed my teaching approach as my understanding of the particular emotional and psychological challenges modern students face has grown. For example, how people can hide from psychological issues in their spiritual practice, as well as sensing the hidden power of our emotional patterns and relational wounding. Such insights have shaped the instructions offered in this book.

My approach as a teacher stems not just from this sensitivity to modern challenges in the emotional and psychological realms but also from my remaining dedicated to the possibility of transformation and awakening. I try to be faithful to the traditional deep wisdom I emerged from, but at the same time being up-to-date and innovative. This means trying to be open and frank in direct interaction with students, while addressing many levels of their tightness, wounding, and confusion at the same time.

When I first started teaching, I used a more traditional style, focusing on theory and emphasizing fine distinctions from traditional texts. Most students were well educated, intellectually grasping the meaning and asking sharp questions. I thought, *Wow, these people are really smart! They should make quick progress.* But after a decade or more, something wasn't feeling quite right. Students were "getting it" up in their heads but seemed stuck in the same emotional and energetic habit patterns year after year. This stuckness prevented them from progressing in their meditation practice.

I began to question whether the approach treasured so much by my tradition was actually touching students in the way intended. I pondered why students around the world were understanding the teachings but not able to embody them and deeply transform.

I suspected that the channels of communication among their minds, their feelings, and their bodies were blocked or strained. From the Tibetan viewpoint all these channels should be connected and flowing freely. Yet I saw that my students couldn't integrate the understanding their intellects were capable of, because they couldn't digest them at the level of the body and feelings. This led me to change how I teach meditation.

Now I focus first and foremost on healing and opening the channel between the mind and the feeling world, to prepare the student's whole being. The techniques described here reflect this new approach, which I've honed for the past few decades. Although they emerge from decades of training with great meditation masters and my own meditation and teaching experience, these are not meant solely for Buddhists or "serious meditators." Quite the contrary, they are designed to benefit anyone and everyone.

Nor are they antidotes to neuroses alone—they offer practical ways to deal with any sort of distressing thoughts and emotions that take us over repeatedly. In addition to fear, these can include aggression, jealousy, unbridled desire, and any other such obstacle to inner peace.

I'm passionate about sharing meditation in a way that is psychologically and emotionally relevant, practical, and accessible to people caught up in today's world. We have precious little time to work with our minds and hearts, so the techniques need to benefit us here and now.

DANIEL GOLEMAN

I grew up in Stockton, California, a town about ninety minutes east of the San Francisco Bay Area. At the time, I experienced the place as Norman Rockwell–ish, a peaceful, Middle American town. Of late, though, Stockton has grown a very different reputation: the first city in America to go bankrupt, as well as the site of an experiment in giving impoverished citizens a monthly stipend—and a hotbed of gangs.

It struck me early in childhood that my friends' houses had almost no books, while my own had thousands. Both my parents were college teachers and valued education as the best path to life success. Just as they had before me, I took school seriously and worked hard at it.

That got me into a college on the East Coast, and from there to Harvard to study for a PhD in clinical psychology. But my education path took a sharp right turn when I received a predoctoral traveling fellowship to India, where I spent two years studying—as I told my sponsors—psycho-ethnology, or "Asian models of the mind." Actually I found myself plunging into the study of meditation.

I had started meditating as an undergrad, and in India enthusiastically undertook a series of ten-day retreats. I found a state of inner peace in those retreats and continued the practice when I returned stateside. Over the decades as a meditator I've encountered a series of marvelous teachers, and today I find myself a student of Tsoknyi Rinpoche.

My dissertation at Harvard was on meditation as an intervention in stress, and I have followed the science of contemplative practice closely ever since. My career path took me into science journalism, eventually to the *New York Times*, where I worked on the science desk. My core skill in this line of work continues to be delving into what scientific journals report and translating those findings in a way that ordinary folks without any special training can understand and find interesting.

That led me to write a book about the scientific findings of meditation with an old friend from my grad school days, Richard Davidson, now a world-renowned neuroscientist based at the University of Wisconsin. Our book, *Altered Traits: Science Reveals How Meditation Changes Your Brain, Body, and Mind*, draws on the soundest studies of meditation practice. I've returned to that well of contemplative science in my contribution to this book, reviewing the findings from the lab that speak to the practices Tsoknyi Rinpoche shares in each chapter.

What This Book Offers You

Mindfulness has been sweeping through our businesses, schools, yoga centers, medical centers, and far beyond, penetrating the distant corners of Western society. While that respite from life's cares understandably appeals to many, mindfulness is just one of many tools in deeper meditation practice. The practice path we detail in this book covers basic mindfulness but also goes far beyond. We tell you what to do next, after you've started mindfulness—as well as what to do at the outset to disarm the deep emotional habits that often propel people to.

This book helps you with widespread obstacles to focusing

we face in that modern life—not just our ever-present phones and increasingly hectic schedules but, even more, the destructive thoughts like doubt and cynicism, and emotional habits like self-criticism that preoccupy us. The early chapters help readers allay the two problems most beginning meditators complain about: (1) *My mind is wild, I can't find calm*, and (2) *My most troubling thoughts just keep coming back*. In an adaptation of meditation instructions to work with these two obstacles, Tsoknyi Rinpoche starts with "dropping," where the meditator cuts through persistent thoughts, and the "handshake," where meditators learn to make friends with their most troubling mental patterns.

These practices, typically missing from standard mindfulness instructions, are invaluable. Many who begin mindfulness abandon the method, frustrated and upset that the thoughts they were trying to overcome continue to bedevil them. This book deals with how to handle such thoughts head-on with love and acceptance.

What's more, several of the methods shared here have not been made widely available before. They are familiar only to Rinpoche's students but so far not to a wider public.

This book is for you:

+ if you have been considering starting meditation and are not sure why you should or how to begin;
+ if you are meditating but wonder why or what to do next to progress;
+ or if you already are a convinced meditator and want to help someone you care about get going, by giving them this book.

TWO

· —— · ✦ · —— ·

DROP IT!

If you *can't* change anything, why worry?
And if you *can* change something, why worry?
—TIBETAN SAYING

TSOKNYI RINPOCHE: THE EXPLANATION

When I was growing up in Nepal and northern India in the seventies and eighties, the pace of life was not too fast. Most people felt quite grounded. Our bodies were loose, and we'd sit down for tea at any time. We smiled easily. Of course we faced plenty of challenges, like poverty and lack of opportunity, but stress and speediness were not really part of the picture.

But as these places slowly developed, the pace of life sped up. There were more and more cars on the road, and more people had jobs with deadlines and expectations. Many people had caught a whiff of middle-class life and wanted a piece of it. I noticed people starting to show signs of stress, physically and mentally. They'd fidget more, their legs quivering nervously under the table. Their gaze was less steady—eyes darting around—and they smiled less freely.

I felt it myself too when I started working on complex projects. I'd started a multiyear initiative to preserve the texts of my lineage, and the project office was across town. I'd wake up and my mind would already be in the office. My feeling world would be hammering me, *Go, go, go! Just one swipe with your toothbrush and spit! Just put the whole breakfast in your mouth, chew once, and swallow! You don't have time for this!*

On my drive across town to my office, the Kathmandu traffic was almost unbearable. *Just step on the gas! Don't worry if you bump someone—doesn't matter! Just get there now!* By the time I walked into the office, I'd feel burned-out already. I'd quickly everyone, not slowing down and taking the time to really check in. I'd want to get out of there as soon as I could.

Ducking out, I'd go somewhere, anywhere—like a coffee shop. Sitting there with nothing particular to do, I'd want to calm down but still felt anxious and restless. My whole being felt like a big buzzy lump—my body, feelings, and mind were all stressed for no reason.

But one day I decided to challenge myself. I would start to respect my body's speed limit, its natural speed, instead of listening to the stubborn, distorted speedy energy. I said to myself, *I will just do everything normally, at the right pace. Whenever I reach my office, I reach my office. I won't let the restless energy push me.*

I went through my morning relaxed, moving at a pace that suited me. I stretched in bed before getting up. I brushed my teeth properly, taking enough time to do it right. When the speedy energy tried to push me—*Go faster, get there now! Grab something for breakfast and eat it in the car!*—I didn't listen.

I was respecting my body's speed limit. Sitting down for breakfast, I chewed properly, tasting my meal. I drove at the appropriate speed, without a sense of rush. I even enjoyed the drive. Whenever the speedy energy told me to go faster—*Just get there*—I smiled and shook my head. In the end, I reached my office almost at the same time as before.

Walking in, I felt fresh and relaxed. The office seemed calmer and more beautiful than I remembered. I sat down and drank tea with my staff, looking each of them in the eyes and really checking in. There was no urge to leave.

Finding Our Ground

I'd like to start from the ground up. In my tradition we like building things—temples, nunneries, monasteries, stupas. Maybe it's a compensation for our nomadic roots. In any case, our metaphors often involve construction. As any builder knows, it's important to have a solid foundation to build on. For meditation, it's also important to have a healthy, solid foundation to begin with.

The raw material is our bodies, minds, and feelings. We're working with our thoughts and emotions—our happiness and sadness, our challenges and struggles. In the case of meditation, a solid foundation means we're grounded, we're present, we're connected. These days, for many reasons, this can be quite tough. So I like to start my own practice, and the practice of my students, with a grounding exercise: a way to find the body, land in the body, connect to the body. The busyness of our thinking minds is seemingly endless and often leaves us feeling anxious, tired, and ungrounded. So this approach is to cut through the whirling thoughts, to bring awareness back into the body, and to just be there for a while. We are reconnecting our minds and our bodies, finding our ground.

The Technique of Dropping

The first technique I'd like to share, *dropping*, works to break the habit of being caught up in our thinking minds—lost in thought—and out of touch with our bodies. *Dropping* is not so much a meditation as a way to temporarily cut through the tension-building stream of constant thinking, worrying, and speediness. It allows us to land in the present moment, in a grounded and embodied way. It gets us ready for meditation.

In dropping you do three things at the same time:

1. Raise your arms and then let your hands drop onto your thighs.

2. Exhale a loud, big breath.

3. Drop your awareness from thinking into what your body feels.

Just rest there, being aware of your body, without any special agenda. Feel your body and all its sensations: pleasant or unpleasant, warmth or coolness, pressure, tingling, pain, bliss, whatever comes into your awareness. It doesn't matter what the feelings are. If you can't feel anything, that's fine too—just be with the numbness.

So in brief: drop, rest, and relax. We're simply letting awareness become grounded in the body. We're not looking for a special state, not looking for a particular feeling. There is no way to get it wrong, because feelings and sensations aren't right or wrong; they just are. Because we have a strong mental habit of popping back up into our heads and losing track of our grounded body, you can try dropping over and over again as you need, to interrupt your thoughts.

Just try it for five minutes at a time: Drop your hands, let a big breath out, and drop your thinking mind into sensing your body. Rest there for a little while, maybe a minute or so, and then drop again. Repeat this over and over as needed.

Let yourself relax from within. Give yourself permission not to do anything. It might feel a little foreign at first, but with practice it gets more natural and uncontrived.

As your awareness settles into your body, notice the grounded quality of the body, its natural earthiness, heaviness, and stillness. Notice its point of contact with the floor or the chair. Allow a sense of the simple calmness of being: it's just your body, an earthy container of flesh, nerves, and bone, sitting here, not doing anything for a while.

Learning to Relax

Relaxation is a funny thing. We all want it, but actually doing it is surprisingly difficult. We often think of relaxing as the opposite of being alert. Being alert and aware is our "on mode" where we get things done, while relaxing is a way to switch off and dim our systems down.

When we think about relaxing we might see ourselves collapsing into a couch with a remote control and becoming mindless. This relaxing into dullness gives some temporary relief but doesn't help the root cause of the stress. The stress lingers underneath, and we end up not feeling as refreshed as we'd hoped.

Dropping is a different approach to relaxing. It's a deeper, inner relaxing, connected to our bodies and feelings, not trying to escape from them and relax somewhere else. Rather than cultivating a dull state as an antidote to stress, we are learning how to relax with awareness and address the root cause of this imbalance where we live lost in our thoughts.

For many beginners in meditation, worrisome thoughts can feel like an unconquerable obstacle—we often hear from people just starting to practice some version of "My mind is out of control. I can't do this!" Dropping targets this universal predicament: our thoughts keep going and can overwhelm our practice.

Dropping gives us a way to clear our mind, if only for moments, so we can start again from a grounded, embodied place. Dropping breaks the tension-building stream of constant thinking, worrying, and speediness and readies us for every other meditation practice, so we begin with that.

◆ · · ◆ · · ◆

Try These Drop-It-All Mantras

It can be helpful sometimes to use a mantra—a phrase you repeat silently to yourself—while doing this dropping practice. There are two mantras I like to use; try them each to see which works best for you. Here's the first one:

Just after your hands hit your lap, say this mantra silently to yourself, or in a whisper, over and over: "So what! Who cares? No big deal."

This sends a message to our anxious, worrying minds. It's a reminder to the part of our minds that cares too much—that holds everything a bit too tightly. Of course caring to the right degree is good and important, but it's too often mixed with extra anxiety and becomes neurotic over-concern. So this mantra is an antidote for all that.

You can also try this one: "Whatever happens, happens. Whatever doesn't happen, doesn't happen." You can repeat this one over and over inside your mind, or try whispering it to yourself if that's helpful.

This message reminds us to be with the flow of experience, instead of trying to control everything. Even though we know this intellectually, we need to remind our feeling bodies. That's where the speediness is held; that's where the stress accumulates.

These mantras have another purpose, to strengthen communication between our cognitive minds and our feeling bodies. As we'll explore in the next technique, this relationship can often be strained—and this can cause problems.

◆

DANIEL GOLEMAN: THE SCIENCE

Growing up in a small city in California, I went to a public high school—but journeyed east to a hypercompetitive private college. There I was stymied by a mandatory freshman-year class in calculus. I had never heard of calculus, a topic far beyond the math taught in my public high school.

And unlike my college classmates, most of whom had attended academically focused prep schools, I had not taken precalculus. In fact, I had also never heard the terms *precalculus* or *prep school*. I got a D in my freshman-year calculus course.

That initial setback triggered surges of anxiety in me about how I would perform in college classes. That chain of worry continued even after I started doing better in my classes. This anxiety seemed disconnected from reality, feeding on itself and ignoring any evidence that might disconfirm it.

That's how toxic worry works. There are three varieties of worry. In the best kind, we worry—that is, focus on and think over and over about a challenge—then come up with some positive step we can take to remedy things and finally drop that train of anxiety. That's *productive* worry.

The second kind of worry crops up when we face a threat or emergency and then dissipates after that situation passes. We focus in a realistic way on a threat. That's *appropriate* worry.

But the worst kind afflicted me: worry that loops over and over in our minds without resolution. Cognitive science calls this *rumination*: worry that keeps going and going, an unstoppable stream of thought. Research at Stanford University finds rumination itself not only generates our worst feelings but also intensifies and prolongs them. At three in the morning we pop up awake as that same worrisome stream immediately seizes our focus. This toxic sort of worry has become ubiquitous these days.

Here's why we worry—it's left over from our earliest ancestors. For much of human prehistory the brain served as the main organ for survival, constantly scanning for danger. This same threat-detection circuitry survives in the human brain and for most of human history was a key to our ancestors' survival: if this vigilant circuitry spotted a threat, that would instantly lead to fighting, fleeing, or freezing to hide in place. At least among those ancestors who survived to pass that reflex on to us. Today those circuits ready our physiology to adjust to a sudden strong reaction and stir us to action—a knee-jerk response we experience today as being flooded by a sudden, intense negative emotion along with the impulse to act.

The amygdala is the brain's radar for threat; at the least sign of danger this circuitry captures the prefrontal cortex—the brain's executive center—and pitches us into feelings like fear or anger. This seems to have worked well in prehistory, when the dangers the amygdala detected were, say, animals that would eat us. But in modern life this design of the brain often fails us, for several reasons.

For one, the amygdala gets a fuzzy signal. While it has superfast one-neuron-long links to eye and ear, most information coming into the brain goes elsewhere. The amygdala sees something like a static-filled TV screen. For another, the amygdala's decision rule is "better safe than sorry"—it makes snap decisions based on poor information. But in modern life the "threats" are rarely physical. Instead they reflect a complex symbolic reality, like *He's not treating me fairly.* Result: the amygdala too often hijacks the executive center in ways that lead us to act in ways we later regret.

The amygdala takes over our attention circuits, making that perceived threat the focus of our attention. When the amygdala triggers, we not only focus our attention on the perceived threat but also keep bringing that danger to mind when our focus wanders off to other thoughts—along with a strong emotional impetus to do something about it. In other words, we worry.

The kind of worry I was lost in during my college days—rumination—is what dropping helps us with. While there are no brain studies of dropping as yet, by inference from what research has found it seems that when we are caught up in ruminative worrying a sudden disruption of these thoughts can clear our minds—much like being startled abruptly ends whatever we were thinking about. And to handle that kind of worry I turned to the path that eventually brought me to study with Tsoknyi Rinpoche.

THREE

·——·◆·——·

BELLY-BREATHING

TSOKNYI RINPOCHE: THE EXPLANATION

If I had to pick one word to capture the most challenging aspect of our modern lifestyle it would be *speediness*. The pace of our home and work lives, combined with how much information and stimulation we receive all the time, can throw off our groundedness and contentment.

Speed, overstimulation, and pressure make us feel more sensitive and vulnerable. Unfortunately, these forces keep hammering our sensitized bodies and minds. Looking more closely into stress, I've noticed that our physical bodies and cognitive minds are not so much the primary problem. We can move only as fast as we can move. We are usually able to think quite fast if we need to. So where is the problem? What gets so stressed out? It's our energetic world—our feelings, emotions, sensations, and flow. It's this gray area, which we often overlook or dismiss, that is key. The Tibetan tradition takes this area of being human quite seriously and offers a range of techniques and insights into how to keep our energy balanced and healthy.

As I mentioned in the last chapter, I've seen the impacts of speediness and stress in my own life and felt it in my body. It built up over time, and it started to affect me. I became curious where the effect was actually happening and even went for a checkup with my doctor. There was nothing physically wrong. As I looked inside, I saw my thinking mind was also fine—still sharp and fast. So what was being impacted so much? I realized that this speediness and stress was most of all impacting my energy and emotions—what I now call my feeling body.

I realized my energy and breath were up in my chest and head instead of down in my belly. This made me feel buzzy, slightly off-balance, and ungrounded. I felt a little pressure in my head and a slight burning in my eyes. I started to feel a little less joy at ordinarily fun things, and started daydreaming about when I could take a day off and do nothing, or when I could next squeeze in a holiday. As I identified this pattern in myself, I started to see it everywhere, in people I encountered and students I taught all over the world.

Luckily I had some background training in working with the body and mind, so I was able to apply techniques to remedy the situation. Once I started sharing these methods, I found people seemed to find them helpful. And so the techniques we share in this chapter are ones that have helped me and many of my friends and students.

◆ · ◆ · ◆

TRY THIS FOR A FEW MOMENTS: Close your eyes and drop your awareness into the body. Be present with whatever is happening. Merely feel how it is. Are you feeling stressed or relaxed? How does that feel? Can you distinguish physical sensations of the body—warm, cool, pain, pleasure, tightness—from more subtle or energetic feelings, such as buzzy, speedy, anxious, excited, calm, and so on? Whatever is happening, don't resist it or worry about it, just feel it.

· ◆ ·

The Three Speed Limits

When I challenged myself that morning in Kathmandu to slow down, the experience of moving at my body's natural speed helped me understand an important distinction between my body, my thinking mind, and my energy. To my surprise, when I looked for the root of the problem—the stress—I couldn't find it in my body or mind. I realized there are three kinds of speed: the physical, the cognitive, and the feeling or energetic. I could walk and move quickly without stress and tension. My body could move however fast it needed to; the problem wasn't there. My mind could think fast and creatively; that was also fine. It was my *feeling world* that was off-balance, distorted. So I realized stress accumulates in the energetic world, the feeling world. The more I understood what was happening inside me, the more I saw it outside as well, all over the world. Whatever we call it—speediness, anxiety, restlessness, stress—I think almost all of us can relate.

I call this understanding the *three speed limits*: the *physical* speed limit, the *mental* speed limit, and the *feeling* or *energetic* speed limit. The body has its own healthy speed, but the feeling world can be rushed in a distorted way. That feeling—of restless, anxious energy—is not healthy. It's distorted because it's not rational; it's out of touch with reality. Speedy energy tells us to get there *now*, even when we can't. Anxiety tells us *we're going to die* when we aren't.

To help distinguish the body's speed limit from the feeling world's speed limit, imagine you have to clean a large room. You walk in and see what needs to be done. Moving furniture, dusting, wiping, and vacuuming—it will take about an hour. This is the physical speed limit. The feeling world, however, can be either relaxed or banging on us the whole time: *Go faster! Finish as soon as possible! I want this to be over!* If we do it like this, we'll feel stressed the whole time and burned-out in twenty minutes. If our energy is relaxed, on the other hand, we can respect our natural speed limit and clean the room the same, without feeling rushed or restless. We might even feel fresh when it's done.

If we don't distinguish between these speed limits, it's as if we haven't diagnosed the problem correctly, and so we can't apply the right remedy. A major misunderstanding is thinking that speedy energy and fast movement are almost the same. Then we either keep trying to slow down our bodies, or slow down our thinking minds. Neither of these works, because the physical and cognitive are not where the problem is, and not where the solution is found either. Not only that but these strategies cause other problems too. If we slow down our bodies and minds, we can start to worry about functioning well in the world. We can also start to be afraid and pull back from the world, as if it were an enemy. But we need to function; life is fast, and we can't slow it down. We have to run in the world. We need to move our bodies, and we need to use our minds. Thinking fast is fine; it's useful! So what is this third part of our being, this murky area of the feeling world? I think it's the key to understanding and working with stress.

✦ · ◆ · ✦

Drop awareness into the body and feel the feelings and energies, whatever they are. If they are speedy or anxious, feel that; if they are relaxed and grounded, feel that. Either sitting or standing, start to shake your body and move your hips, shoulders, and arms, like you're dancing to your favorite song. Play with moving while internally tense and moving while relaxed from within. See what these feel like. See if you can move normally, even quickly, without there being any tension inside.

· ◆ ·

Energy and the Subtle Body

In the Tibetan tradition we call this murky feeling world the *subtle body*. We call the energy that flows through it *lung* (pronounced "loong"), which is roughly equivalent to *chi* in the Chinese or *prana* in the Indian traditions. For lack of a better term in English, we can call it *energy*. The *subtle body*, which is the world of feelings and energies, operates between the cognitive mind and the physical body. In traditional Tibetan yogic physiology, the subtle body is composed of *prana* (energies), *nadi* (channels), and *bindu* (essences). The *nadi*, or channels, are the "structure," and are more or less equivalent to the meridians in traditional Chinese medicine, which is how acupuncture works. Our channels can be knotted or smooth, blocked or open. Our *prana*, or energies, flow through these channels and can be trapped or free-flowing, dysregulated or balanced. Our *bindu*, or essences, are like seeds of joy, bliss, inspiration, clarity, and love. (We'll come back to the *bindu* in a later chapter.)

What's most relevant here is the *prana*, the energies. The *prana* is strongly connected to the breath. In fact, another way to refer to *prana*, or *lung*, is "winds." The breath is even considered a type of coarse physical *prana*. It affects the subtler internal energies. When we breathe shallow or roughly, such as when we're startled or anxious, it elevates the tension, the energy of the mood or emotion. When we breathe deeply and smoothly, it helps regulate and soothe the internal energies.

One of our main energies is called the *upward-moving energy* in the Tibetan system. It is the energy that rises when we need to act, to respond, to move quickly, to think fast, to get stuff done. It's very useful in daily life and in emergencies, this ability to respond quickly to dynamic situations. In a healthy system, once the *upward-moving energy* has done its work, it returns to its natural resting place below the navel, and we can relax and restore.

When this energy becomes chronically overstimulated, however, it stops returning to its natural resting place. It can get stuck in the upper parts of the body—the head, neck, shoulders, chest, and upper back. It keeps buzzing around in the upper body and keeps hammering us. Then we start to feel the symptoms of chronic stress. Some common physical signs are sensitive, watery eyes; dry mouth and lips; headaches; tension in our necks and shoulders; and buzzing in our chests. We can feel vulnerable, chickenhearted, off-balance, and ungrounded. The speedy energy also triggers restless, anxious thoughts.

One way to imagine this is as a three-story house. The first floor is the physical body, the second floor is the energy or feeling world, and the top floor is the mind. When the second floor, the world of feelings and energies, is imbalanced, it keeps banging "upward" on the mind, triggering those restless, anxious thoughts. It also keeps banging "downward" on the body, triggering various symptoms of stress. When the second floor is balanced and calm, we can move our bodies fast, think quickly and creatively—and still remain relaxed and healthy. The second floor of feelings and energies is where we accumulate stress and where we can learn to be calm.

TRY THIS: Drop awareness into the body and feel the feelings and energies. Be a little curious. Where is the energy? What is the energy? What is speedy? We are not inviting an experience so much as searching, discovering something that is already there.

The challenge comes when we go over our natural speed limit in the feeling world. Modern life moves fast, and we cram more and more in at younger ages. My daughter was juggling school-work, exams, deadlines, hobbies, transportation, and social media, and this was when she was still a teenager. If we add a job and a family, the pressure and busyness can just pile up more. These external pressures are internalized into our sensitive systems.

We repeatedly go over our natural speed limit to keep up and stay on top of things, generating anxious hopes and fears. We all too often just keep rushing, keep pushing. With subconscious fears of falling behind or falling apart, we ignore messages from our feeling world to slow down, to take a break, or make a change. All this leads to our natural groundedness being compromised.

In the previous chapter we learned dropping as a way to drop out of our thinking minds and land in our bodies. Much unnecessary stress can melt away with this technique, if we practice it again and again. It can help us feel more grounded and embodied. But not all of our stress can be dropped so easily. Some forms of stress have become more deeply established in our bodies, minds, and feeling worlds—we call these *habitual patterns*. When we go over our natural speed limit many times—in school, at work, at home—eventually it becomes a subconscious habit or pattern to be in a state of imbalance.

Over time this can become an energetic disorder—what in the West might be called ongoing anxiety: We find we cannot calm down inside even when we want to. Even when our coarse body is relaxed, inside something is moving. We try to relax that, but we can't turn it off. We keep buzzing. It's like an engine in neutral but with the gas pedal pushed down. The car is revving, but we aren't going anywhere. Many of us have experienced lying in bed at night when we should be relaxing and falling asleep but just can't. *Mmmmmmmmmm*—humming or buzzing energy moves all around our body; we toss and turn restlessly, thinking about work, worrying about this and that. This signifies a residue of disordered, imbalanced energy. This is what we need to work with, to retrain, to transform. The practices here are focused on how to calm our energy down. This is like a secret key to unraveling stress.

Speediness, stress, anxiety, and restlessness are not rooted in the mind—a quick mind is no problem. Moving the body fast is also no problem. We need to *understand* when we're speedy, *feel* the speedy energy, and work with our *breath* to rebalance it. If we do this, one day we will find the balance in our energy. We will see clearly the distinction between the three speed limits and how to care for them. We will learn how to slow down the feeling world but also realize that the body and the mind don't need to slow down. Then we can walk fast but be calm. We can think fast and very creatively, but our energy remains calm. This is the goal.

Think of a kung fu master—Bruce Lee is my favorite. Kung fu masters can move very fast, and their minds have to be sharp and alert, but if they're good, they stay calm. Our energy is naturally calm and intelligent. With that as a basis, our body and mind move. If our energy is speedy, we have symptoms like anxiety and restlessness. If our energy is balanced, then the chance of getting speedy, restless, and anxious is much less. Even if we get speedy we recover much faster. This is why it's so important to distinguish between healthy and unhealthy energy. We need healthy energy to deal with the world.

With these breathing-awareness techniques, one day we will find synchronization. We'll become skilled at working with our energy. We'll be very adept at which part of ourselves to relax and which to enhance. In other words, we'll know how to move the physical, the mental, and the feeling worlds. We'll know how much speed and how much slowness is beneficial. Like a skilled dancer choreographing movement, stillness, rhythm, and expression, we'll become skilled at balancing all these aspects. Then life becomes really enjoyable. The energy and feeling worlds are very relaxed, the mind is clear and open, and the body moves smoothly and sleekly. When nothing pressures us, all our activity becomes a dance, a celebration.

The Practice

There are four gentle breathing techniques that are especially useful for handling this upward-moving energy. These methods retrain the energy to come down below the navel—its natural home—and rest there. They stand alone as beneficial practices and can also be practiced together as a more comprehensive training. They are:

1. Deep belly-breathing, or "baby-breathing."
2. Scanning the body and feeling our speedy energy.
3. Connecting speedy energy and awareness with the breath and bringing them all down below the navel.
4. An extrasubtle method that mainly uses intention with minimal muscle control.

Method #1: Deep Belly-Breathing, or Baby-Breathing

Usually when we're startled, emotionally activated, or just stressed, we breath more quickly, shallowly, and more in our chests. This happens subconsciously but over time can become a habit, and our bodies forget our natural, relaxed way of breathing. In my tradition, we believe the natural way is deep.

◆ · ◆ · ◆

Find a relaxed position to work with your breath. This can be sitting or lying down. If you're sitting, whether on the floor or in a chair, try to find a posture where your back is straight but not tight, upright but relaxed. The position of your hands and feet is not so important; all our bodies are different. Try postures and see which allows you to feel straight but relaxed. Whichever position you take, the most essential point is to be relaxed.

TIP: *If you are sitting in a chair, try either crossing your legs in the chair or sitting in a way that your feet are flat on the floor. If you can't do this, don't worry. If you are lying down, try on your back with a straight spine and, if you can, your legs bent, with your feet flat on the floor.*

Next, put your hands on your lower belly. Your thumbs should be roughly at the level of your navel. Relax your shoulders and arms. Start breathing gently from your abdomen, allowing your belly and hands to rise and fall with each breath. You can rest awareness with the rise and fall of your belly and hands. Try to completely relax your neck, shoulders, and chest so they have no tension. Allow the upper body to fully rest, and let the lower abdomen do most of the movement.

TIP: *If you have trouble finding the breath in your abdomen or relaxing with it, try lying down on your back with your legs bent and feet flat on the floor. Put a medium-size heavy object like a big book on your belly. Feel it gently rise and fall as you practice belly-breathing. This can help settle your body and awareness in this practice.*

When you feel relaxed and are breathing in a regular rhythm, breathe more deeply, letting the belly and hands rise and fall with each breath. Then introduce short pauses when the breath is fully inside and the breath is fully outside. In other words, after exhaling, pause a few seconds before beginning the next inhalation. At the end of the inhalation, hold the breath in for a few seconds before beginning the exhalation. These pauses, just holding for a few seconds, should be relaxed and comfortable. Don't hold until you feel short of breath or strained. This is not a competition, and more is not necessarily better. This is a gradual training, and we are just exploring a new way of breathing.

TIP: *One day you can feel which pause is more helpful, the holding in or holding out. Whichever is for you, do that. Progress comes over time as we feel more and more comfortable holding our breath, and the retention lengthens naturally.*

Finally, just keep relaxing and continuing this belly-breathing. Allow your body to enjoy the deep rhythmic abdominal breathing. Allow your whole system to calm down and let go, like a baby resting without a care in the world. Continue for as long as you are comfortable. This method of deep abdominal breathing has many benefits even without the subsequent techniques.

◆

Method #2: Body-Scanning

The aim of *body-scanning* is to find and connect with our speedy energy, with our feelings of anxiety or restlessness. It's important to bring an attitude of gentleness and curiosity here. Otherwise we can start thinking of our speediness as an enemy or a negative disease that needs to be eliminated. Instead we treat it with tenderness, like an overexcited child. This method is a little different from other traditional body-scanning techniques—for example, those that focus on choiceless awareness—because here we are choosing to pay attention to speedy energy. As with the first technique, this body-scanning technique has many benefits on its own but also serves as an important preparation for the third practice, *khumbak*, or gentle vase breathing.

Begin by finding a comfortable posture, where your spine is straight but your whole body is relaxed. This can be sitting or lying down. Start with a dropping practice for a few breaths, and if you have time, maybe a few minutes of deep.

Then bring awareness to your energetic feeling body and explore to find the speedy energy. There are two ways to scan; by moving awareness through the body or by directly bringing awareness to where it's needed. If you already know where the speedy energy is, you can just go directly there. If not, you can move awareness relaxedly through your head, face, neck, shoulders, upper back, and chest. Remember to be curious and gentle. The main focus is just connecting directly to sensations and feelings; there is no other agenda to this step. We are not looking for particular sensations or feelings, or trying to change our experience

at this point. We are just exploring the of speediness and
restlessness.

———————————— ◆ ————————————

The sensations and feelings associated with speedy energy
can be quite subtle. As you explore more you may notice coarser
physical sensations like tightness, pain, heat, and dryness, as well
as more subtle sensations of tingling, vibrating, and buzzing.
Continue this practice, scanning again and again, just being curious and open to whatever you feel.

Method #3: Gentle Vase Breathing with Retention

This method is a gentler version of a classic technique called *vase
breathing*. Although this modified version is suitable for unsuper-
vised practice, please follow the instructions carefully and listen
to your body.

Gentle vase breathing is where everything comes together. We
build on our skills of belly-breathing and body-scanning, and
learn to bring breath, speedy energy, and awareness together and
hold them under the navel. This practice needs to be repeated
over and over again, because we are *retraining an energetic habit*.
It's very important that the body remain relaxed and the pressure be *very gentle*; if we tense up and push too hard, the practice can backfire and make our energy more unbalanced. If we're

too tight, especially in the upper-stomach area around the solar plexus and sternum, the energy can feel like its blocked, "bouncing" back up into our chest and head. This can actually make us feel temporarily worse.

This is a subtle practice; you'll have to play with it to find the right balance. We can use two main metaphors to help visualize and understand this practice: *the French press* and *the balloon*. These two techniques may yield different experiences, so play with them and see which feels more natural and beneficial for you.

✦ · ◆ · ✦

Begin by taking a posture with the spine straight but the whole body relaxed, either sitting or lying down. Start by doing a few minutes of to prepare the body. Then scan for the speedy energy—signs of restlessness, anxiety, or buzz. When you feel you have connected to the energy, move on to the next step.

THE FRENCH PRESS: Remaining relaxed and grounded, breathe out completely. While breathing in through your nostrils, imagine the breath is mingling with the speedy, restless energy and gently pressing it down, like a French press gently pushing the coffee grounds down to the bottom of the vessel. The speedy energy is being urged from the upper body down through the stomach, to its natural home below the navel. Then hold the breath down there for a few seconds.

The energy needs to be held in the "vase," so we press *very gently* downward with the muscles we use to poop, to hold it all down there. You don't need to push hard. Exhale completely, then inhale and repeat over and over again.

THE BALLOON: This is essentially the same practice physically, but some people find the French press image too forceful and they push too hard. So instead of a French press, imagine there is a balloon in your lower belly, under your navel. In this version, we don't imagine pushing anything down from above. Each breath in fills the balloon, and each breath out empties the balloon.

◆

Remaining relaxed and grounded, breathe out completely, emptying the balloon. As you breathe in, imagine the empty balloon sucking down the breath and speedy energy and filling up below the navel. When it's full, gently "pinch" the top of the balloon to prevent the energy from escaping, by pressing down very gently the muscles we use to poop. Hold the breath for a few seconds. Exhale fully and repeat, over and over.

◆

When holding your breath in like this, it's important not to hold it until you feel strain and gasp for breath. Just start with a few seconds, and gradually build up the duration over days and weeks. If you keep practicing regularly, your capacity will naturally increase, without forcing it. If you start with two to three seconds, for example, you can build it up to ten seconds, and then fifteen to twenty seconds over time.

This is very beneficial, because the increased retention is often a sign of more relaxation in the subtle body, and of more control of the energies.

If you feel tightness in your head or chest, light-headed, or dizzy, you may be tensing up, pushing too hard, or holding the breath too long. Stop the practice and relax for a while. Try practicing gentle belly-breathing and body-scanning to see where the tension is building up. Try to relax that.

Method #4: The Extra-Gentle Way

This final method is for when we have gained some proficiency in the other techniques. When we have become comfortable with belly-breathing, can connect to our speedy energy with awareness, and can regularly bring our speedy energy down to rest in its natural home below the navel, we can try this fourth technique. We have created a link between energy and awareness, and can now use that link to bring speedy energy down with almost no effort. We may notice that the previous techniques are really helpful, but when we get up and have to do other things, our speedy energy pops back up and becomes activated. After all, we can't talk and engage normally if we're holding our breath! This technique helps to bridge these practices with daily life. It allows us to maintain some benefits while talking, moving around, working, and engaging in our lives.

Start by just mentally connecting to the energy in the body and exhaling. While inhaling, imagine bringing breath, energy, and awareness down under the navel. Once you have applied a slight amount of muscular engagement, almost a reminder to the body, keep about 10 percent of your energy and breath down in the "vase," and breathe naturally in and out on top, keeping the chest and shoulders relaxed and natural. Just be as natural and normal as possible. This practice is so subtle no one needs to know you're doing it.

At first, we will be constantly distracted by life and lose this subtle practice. So whenever we lose it, we just need one breath to connect again. Just repeat over and over. Gradually we are forming a new habit, and it becomes easier and easier. We will feel more grounded throughout the day. We will notice many situations that were stressful before become easier to manage. This is really helpful for long meetings!

DANIEL GOLEMAN: THE SCIENCE

My wife and I were in a taxi with Tsoknyi Rinpoche on the way to the Delhi train station. It was March 2000, and we had reservations on a train that would take us up toward Dharamshala, where I would moderate a meeting with the Dalai Lama and a handful of psychologists on the topic of "Destructive Emotions."

We had left with plenty of time to spare, but gridlocked traffic was eating away at the time buffer. I was, frankly, getting uptight, increasingly worried about missing the train—a destructive emotion had taken control.

My anxiety boiled over when our taxi stopped for a red light at the intersection of two huge avenues, which looked less like streets and more like parking lots packed with cars (and the occasional oxcart, bicycle rickshaw, and cow). The red light stopped us for what seemed like an endless amount of minutes.

A silver-colored word in the middle of that red light—*relax*—made no difference in my state. I could not relax, but got more and more tense. My head spun with the swarming colors, sounds, and smells whirling around us like a hurricane. Though our lanes weren't moving anywhere, drivers all around us were showing their impatience in a rising cacophony of honking. I felt a mounting sense of urgency at the traffic jam, an impossible pretzel that had no rhyme nor reason and seemed would never untangle.

"Oh man!" I said to Rinpoche. "This traffic is really snarled. I'm starting to worry about getting to the train."

Rinpoche said, in a soft, calm voice, "Can you feel the speediness? Can you find where it is?"

I closed my eyes and scanned my body, noticing a buzz of sensations and a growing tightness in my belly. I nodded.

Rinpoche continued, "Find it. Feel it. It's not you. It's not your mind, not your body. It's your energy."

Rinpoche added, "First just sense that you are speedy—what that feels like in your body. Then understand that you are tuning into the feeling world. Find where in your body you feel your energy's speediness. Then breathe in and hold the breath down under your navel for as long as is comfortable for you. Exhale slowly, holding back about ten percent of the air."

Getting what he was saying, I took a deep breath and let the air out slowly.

Rinpoche led me through several breaths this way. And, almost miraculously, my tension eased. The light changed, traffic moved again, and I felt more relaxed.

Right on the spot, Rinpoche was guiding me to use the body scan and the gentle vase breathing method. As we've just learned, that gentle vase breathing is one of several ways to work with our breath to calm our nervous energy.

These breath-control practices are ancient in India, and made their way from there, along with Buddhism, to Tibet in the ninth to eleventh centuries. Several such breath-control practices have been preserved and are still taught in various corners of Tibetan Buddhism to this day.

Their purpose: calming the mind for meditation. Science agrees.

It turns out there is sound research showing the power of these breath methods. In recent decades scientists have turned their attention to such breath-control methods, realizing that using them has powerful impacts on our mental state. In short, managing our breath helps us manage our mind.

Key parts of the brain's emotional circuitry get triggered by the amygdala, our neural radar for threat. In today's stressful life our amygdala fires far more often than needed, and the speediness we are caught up in adds to our stress.

That pitches us into "sympathetic nervous system" activity, where our body prepares for an emergency: our heart rate jumps, as does blood pressure; our bronchial passages enlarge, and we breathe faster; our digestion shuts down; blood shifts from our organs to our arms and legs (the better to fight or run); and we sweat.

Such emergency responses are triggered by hormones like adrenaline and cortisol, which mobilize all these systems to prepare for emergency. This biological reaction gets set off all too often these days (*That irksome too-slow driver! That scary fast driver! Difficulty with the kids! That horrible boss!*).

Once stress hormones surge through us, we're more readily triggered for a further stress reaction. And, as we've discussed, these days this threat reaction triggers in response to symbolic threats too—like the feeling that someone is treating us unfairly—not just the physical survival emergency the reaction was designed for. Being treated unfairly feels bad, of course. But it's not the threat to our very life that our fight-or-flight response was designed to handle. Even so, that biological machinery for physical survival also takes over when we undergo a psychological threat like unfair treatment.

We can undergo this fight-or-flight response many times in a single day, all too often without having time to end it. And such a prolonged, ongoing fight-or-flight reaction overtaxes our biology with long-term costs, such as heightened inflammation, lowered immune system defenses, and becoming more susceptible to a range of stress-worsened illnesses.

During the emergency mode our attention shifts to focus on the presumed threat—even when we're trying to get something else more important done, we stay preoccupied by what upsets us. The response is so strong that we might find ourselves thinking about that threat and how to handle it even when we at two a.m. As we read in chapter 2 this kind of anxious worry serves no useful purpose. Some of us might get sad or angry, while others panic. There's no set response, but none of the likely reactions help us.

Contrast that with a "parasympathetic response," the physiological state where the body rests and recovers from such stress. Our heart rate and blood pressure subside and our breath slows, as do the other biological upshifts of the emergency reaction. Our digestion resumes its usual workings. This is the biological state where the body rests, restores itself, and relaxes. We can eat, have sex, sleep.

The body's emergency response has a beginning—when we're triggered—a peak in the middle, and an end, if we have the chance to calm down again. That's what the controlled breathing method Rinpoche offers here does for us: it ends the stress cycle we're caught up by.

Meditation as Stress Reduction

I had the benefits of yogic practices like these breath-control meth-ods in mind when I came back to Harvard from fifteen months in India, where I met many, many cooled-out practitioners of Asian mind-training methods. I was convinced, having been with these seasoned yogis, lamas, and other such teachers, that they were on to something important, a method for managing our minds that contemporary psychology was oblivious to.

At the time, the early 1970s, I was in a graduate program at Harvard in clinical psychology that was dominated by a psychoanalytic view of the mind, and faculty members were not very open to other views. My professors were downright close-minded when it came to anything regarding conscious-ness, especially from the East. This was driven home when my fellow graduate student Richard Davidson proposed doing his dissertation research on Eastern methods of mind training and was told point-blank that doing so would be a "career-ending" move.

I, too, wanted to do such a study for my dissertation. But I would have to find a committee of Harvard faculty who would evaluate and vouch for my work—and most of my professors weren't interested. But my one ally on the faculty, David Mc-Clelland, somehow found a physician at Harvard Medical School who was willing to sit on my committee. That was Dr. Herbert Benson, a cardiologist.

Dr. Benson had done a preliminary study showing that medi-tation seemed to lower blood pressure, an effect of great interest to cardiology. Dr. Benson was to pursue this finding much further and later wrote a book called *The Relaxation Response,* which became a bestseller. The "relaxation response" was a more reader-friendly way of talking about "parasympathetic nervous system arousal" (admittedly, quite a mouthful).

Dr. Benson described what has by now become common knowledge but was newly discovered in those days: how during the relaxation response the body moves into a state of deep relaxation that allows that biological mode of recovery from the emergency arousal of the fight-or-flight mode.

Dr. Benson saw Eastern practices that trigger the relaxation response as a nonmedical intervention that could help people who suffer from a wide range of stress-exacerbated medical problems like hypertension, asthma, and many others. His interest focused on mental methods like meditation, which he removed from their original spiritual context and made available to anyone regardless of their religious faith (or absence of one).

Similar mind-training methods in Eastern traditions were most often accompanied by breath-control techniques, though Dr. Benson did not explore these. Scientists have only recently begun to study what happens in the brain and body during methods where we control our breath—specifically, to slow it down. Stress and anxiety, of course, speed up our breath rate.

In general, studies looking at the impacts of slowed breathing on our brain, mind, and body find a strong shift to the parasympathetic mode. That would have been no surprise to a yogi a millennia or two ago (once you explained the sympathetic and parasympathetic modes to them)—this shift has been a reason for including breath-control methods as part of an array of spiritual practices since ancient times.

There are several ways we can control our breath: slowing it down, inhaling more deeply, changing how long we exhale versus how long we inhale among.

◆ · · ◆ · · ◆

You might be trying these out as you read this—and if not, I encourage you to do so now. Just experiment with how taking control of your breath can change your mental or physical state. We've just learned four methods that use these variations on our natural breath to work with our speedy energy.

◆ ·

Ancient methods for breath control, called *pranayama* in Sanskrit, used all of these breath-control approaches in one way or another. Modern research on breath control has taken these methods out of their spiritual context and into the lab to investigate what benefits there might be from such manipulations for wellness, health, relaxation, and fighting stress. In doing so, scientists have had to disentangle breath control per se from the mind training, hatha yoga, and other such practices it has traditionally been paired with.

The strictest review of scientific findings on breath control examined the benefits from slowing the breath to ten breaths or fewer per minute—the normal range is around twelve to sixteen per minute. The review excluded studies of methods that do not involve controlling the breath, such as mindfulness of breathing, where a person simply becomes aware of breathing without trying to change it. Also excluded were studies where people reported how they felt; scientists see such self-reports as less trustworthy than objective measures like brain waves, which are not susceptible to bias from expectations.

Slowing breathing to six breaths per minute had striking effects on heart rate variability, an index of physical fitness measured by the time between each of heartbeat. Our heart beat rate results from the interplay of many biological forces. Two main ones are the fight-or-flight mode, which speeds up heart rate, and the relaxation mode, which slows it down. In the hectic pace of modern life, people tend to have a faster heart rate, which means a smaller between-beat interval.

Perhaps counterintuitively, having alternatively longer and shorter between-beat gaps indicates a biological readiness to adapt to changing demands. The difference in gap time results from this ongoing tug-of-war between the sympathetic and parasympathetic branches of the nervous system. If we have little difference in these gap times when we are at rest, this usually means one branch, typically the fight-or-flight, has taken over, which indicates constant stress. So the scientists doing the review suggest that having a variation in the time between heartbeats indicates a healthy relaxation mode, possibly one biological driver of the positive changes slow breathing seems to bring. One study of slow breathing sees this increase in heart rate variability as a doorway to optimal neural and biological functioning—a state of "alert relaxation."

To summarize all the studies: Along with this healthy variability in time between heartbeats, people doing slowed breathing reported feeling ease and comfort, being more relaxed, as well as having positive energy and a general feeling of pleasantness. Such results were found when people slowed their breath to ten per minute, though the benefits were better at six per minute—and both slowed rates had greater health advantages than did normal breathing.

Slowed breathing also seems to bring a significant change in brain function. Electroencephalography (EEG) studies found that slower breathing was accompanied by an increase in synchronized alpha waves, which signify the brain has gone into a state of rest, like a car idling. This shift in brain state was associated with benefits like lessened anxiety, anger, and confusion, and an increase in feelings of vigor.

While there are so far too few research studies to say with certainty, slow breathing seems to drive our brain and our cardiac and respiratory systems into the "relaxation response," that mode of recovery, restoration, and relaxed alertness. And that was what I had sensed in those contemplative masters I encountered during my time in India—and what Tsoknyi Rinpoche showed me when I got so uptight at that stoplight in Delhi.

FOUR

. —— . ✦ . —— .

BEAUTIFUL MONSTERS

TSOKNYI RINPOCHE: THE EXPLANATION

As a young child in Nepal and then in India from age thirteen on-ward, I was educated by Tibetan Buddhist lamas, a deeply privi-leged and nourishing way to grow up. Physical conditions were quite basic in those days, but the human side was very rich. I was surrounded by warm, kind, and brilliant mentors, and I looked up to them in so many ways. They taught me useful tools to deal with my mind, my life, and my work.

As I became a teenager, however, I began to observe and feel new kinds of emotional patterns and inner struggles. I was in an intense study program and had started late, and was playing a bit of catch-up. I was studying a classic text about good and evil thoughts and their dire consequences, and it advised a close examination of each thought that arose in my mind. As I intensely watched thought after thought I became terrified and obsessed. I saw so many negative thoughts, and I couldn't control them! One judgment after another, one afflictive emotion after another, just kept filling my mind. I was acutely aware of each one, and increasingly horrified by the negative karma I thought I was accumulating. I was also judging myself harshly for having these negative thoughts and emotions in the first place, and I felt trapped in a negative-feedback loop. I became unbalanced and a little neurotic. It was a very uncomfortable space to be in, and it lasted for months.

Fortunately, after the end of the school year I was able to travel back to my family and get instruction from my father that helped me come out of that space. The experience taught me some valuable lessons. I learned that mindfulness can go wrong! I was mindful of every thought but didn't know what to do with them. Just noticing, just being mindful, is not enough. Its good, but we need more. Mindfulness is a powerful tool, but it needs to be complemented with other qualities to be balanced, to become an actual path. For example, I learned we need loving kindness, patience, insight, and integrity. Without these, mindfulness could be harnessed for anything—to become a more effective liar or a better manipulator, or to harm people. Within ourselves, being mindful of thoughts and emotions is a good first step, but without some technique, insight, and perspective, there is no guarantee we will work with them skillfully.

Later, as an older teenager and a young man, I also faced the challenge of massive pressures and expectations. We monk-lamas were held to almost impossibly high standards. If we internalized them, which many of us did, it was almost enough to freeze you into a ball of tension. We were expected to act almost perfectly, like an idealized hero out of the life stories of our predecessors, who were often renunciants and lived in premodern times. We were expected to have virtually no personal needs and yet shoulder big responsibilities as soon as we finished our studies in our late teens or early twenties. These were complex and sometimes conflicting expectations. For example, we were expected to be capable managers and fundraisers for our monasteries and nunneries and yet not be "worldly." I had to work with these pressures and find a way to hold all of this—to honor my responsibilities and yet also somehow be natural, relaxed, and free, qualities that are essential for the practice of my lineage teachings.

As I began to travel and teach as a young adult, the people I met were facing different cultural and educational conditioning than what we Tibetans were accustomed to. I realized that to be an effective meditation teacher and really benefit people from cultures different than my own, I had to learn about their particular emotional and psychological patterns. I sought out people I could talk to and learn from, especially practitioners of Western psychology and psychotherapy. I wanted to know how they understood their patterns, and how they worked with them.

One longtime friend of mine in particular whom I learned

from is the psychotherapist. We talked for hours on many occasions about psychological schemas—emotional patterns—how they form and how they can be healed. I challenged her on certain beliefs, and she challenged me right back. I realized from these dialogues that some of modern psychotherapy's insights can complement our traditional Buddhist understanding of emotional patterns, wounding, and healing. For example, I would describe certain traditional ways of seeing emotions and how to work with them. She acknowledged these perspectives and techniques as valid but expressed her concerns about the sensitivity and woundedness many modern people feel. She tried to convince me that the woundedness can be a very significant challenge and needs special gentleness to heal. At first I was unsure, but slowly I appreciated her ideas more and more. I began to notice some of the emotional hindrances that were getting in the way of my students' spiritual practice.

Traditionally we talk about karmic seeds and temporary conditions combining to form our experience, with all of its ups and downs. Karmic seeds are imprints left by physical, verbal, and mental actions that are stored in our consciousness and ripen into various experiences when the causes and conditions are right. This is correct so far as it goes, but therapists describe relational and emotional development from childhood onward in great detail and with many nuances. I began to realize that many peoples' patterns cut them off from their own feeling world, while others who are more in touch feel a strained relationship at best. The mind so often judges and tries to control the feeling world. Schemas, patterns, relational wounding, traumas—these concepts have helped refine my understanding of our emotional worlds and also helped me adapt traditional meditation techniques to be more relevant.

When I was having that problem with negative thoughts as a teenager, it was not just about thoughts; it was coming from a deeper issue in the feeling world. At the time I was dealing with it mainly as a mind issue, not working with the feelings underneath. I didn't have a good understanding of the feeling world and how it works—how so many thoughts are rooted in the feeling world. The instructions, love, and care from my father, Tulku Urgyen Rinpoche, helped me come out of that teenage dilemma. And later, in those talks with Tara, I realized that while many of us have our big problems with thoughts, the root is often really in the feeling world, which is not well taken care of. I learned a language for how to talk about this area of our experience, where thoughts and feelings meet.

So it's time to talk about our issues in this chapter, to get more real. Everybody has issues—if you don't suffer, you're not normal. I've met a few people who claimed not to have any emotional struggles, but they just numb to me. We all have some bruises, some scrapes from our early years.

Some of our issues we can call *wounded love*—we didn't get the love and respect we feel we needed. Maybe the love we did receive was conditional, given only when we performed well. Maybe we even started to believe we were unworthy of love. These types of experiences affect us. They affect our relationships with others and our relationship with ourselves. They can lead to patterns of resistance and reaction, and either way it makes it difficult to feel grounded in our warm hearts, to be fully present with ourselves and others in a healthy way. There are other issues, of course—all kinds of anxieties, depressions, and neurotic thinking and judging.

Raw feelings and emotions can be overwhelming, scary, and powerful; we fear we might lose control. So we often suppress, hide, or run away. In some ways this strategy can be sensible, practical, and functional: it's a rare meeting that can be interrupted to spend twenty minutes with our eyes closed, feeling subtle tender spots, and softly weeping. Suppressing or ignoring are coping strategies and can help us through a challenging situation, but they're short-term solutions. With our difficult feelings ignored, our minds can stay busy with planning and accomplishing tasks. We hope the feelings will just go away over time, or if they don't we tell ourselves we'll deal with them later sometime. But then when we do have time to relax, we don't feel like dealing with our stuff, so we distract and numb ourselves in countless ways.

Our issues may be kept under the surface, but they still affect us. Situations and relationships keep triggering them, requiring continuous energy to suppress or run away from them. When we avoid facing our difficult feelings, this can lead to an unhealthy relationship between our minds and our feeling worlds. Many people just slowly go numb. For others their minds can become like controlling, judging bosses, and their feelings like angry, hurt teenagers acting out.

Over time a sad thing can happen: our innate birthright, a natural well-being on the feeling level, an okayness for no reason, can get covered up. Instead of feeling that spark of dignity—which

I call *essence love*—we can feel a hollowness. When hollowness is underneath our feeling world, we become subconsciously devoted to filling it. Many things we do, from our spiritual practices to our self-care routines to our relationships, can be tainted by a secret hidden agenda to fill the hollowness.

Authentic and Distorted Relative Experience

The *relative* truth is everything we normally experience, all the changing content of our experience, all our concepts and perceptions and emotional patterns—all our pain and pleasure, joys and struggles, our wounding and healing. We call it *relative* because it always depends on conditions interacting, and we can break it down in many ways, analyzing and interpreting.

For example, to say "you hurt my feelings" is fine at the surface level. It's something we say routinely and it means something similar to many of us, so it's functional. But when we look more deeply, things get more complex. Actually, many causes and conditions had to come together for my feelings to be hurt. I may have had to think you intended it; I may have had to be primed somehow from the past for that hurting; the nature of our relationship may have yielded expectations; I may have misunderstood something you said or did; I may have reacted in a way that played an important role in feeling hurt, and so on. So although "hurt feelings" really happened, the solid unexamined belief "you hurt my feelings" is true only in a surface sense.

Relative truth has two dimensions: *functional*, *authentic* relative truth and *distorted, deceptive* relative perception. This is an important distinction. The main focus for us here is healing the distorted into the healthy. We all have different programs, some healthy and some not so healthy. For example, many people struggle with the pattern of seeing themselves as unworthy. This is a distorted program; nobody is fundamentally unworthy. Yet this program can be triggered by many situations and in all kinds of relationships, making us feel and think in a way that is unhealthy. This is the sort of thing that can be healed into the healthy relative truth.

Traditionally we talk about *karmic* and *learned habitual patterns*. *Karmic patterns* are imprints deep within our consciousness, the core tendencies to believe in a solid sense of self, to feel emotions like passion, aggression, jealousy, and pride. We talk of these karmic seeds or imprints carrying on from lifetime to lifetime, but whether you believe this or not, its beneficial to understand that these patterns are tenacious and unconscious.

Learned habitual patterns are what we accumulate from childhood in this life. These arise from our formative social and emotional experiences, our relationships with our relatives and friends and teachers, at home and in school. These lead to internalized beliefs about ourselves and others, and patterns of behavior, such as resisting and reacting to certain situations and emotions. Working with beliefs can be tricky because subconscious attitudes are stubborn: "It's shameful to be angry." "It was unacceptable to show anger when I was a child." "I learned men don't show their feelings and never cry." "I was raised to think that being emotional was a sign of weakness."

Beautiful Monsters

All of us have some issues, challenging emotional patterns that make our lives and relationships more difficult. It might be unworthiness, or a particular kind of fear, or self-righteousness, or envy, or some kind of irrational anger. There are many possibilities. We often feel ashamed and irritated by our issues. We resist and react to them, sometimes we hate them. Usually, we just wish they would go away. I like to call them *beautiful monsters*.

Beautiful monsters are patterns of reaction that are slightly or greatly distorted. For example, if we felt undervalued or underappreciated as a kid, we might overreact as an adult to ordinary criticism or blame. This overreaction is a beautiful monster.

Both parts of this phrase *beautiful monsters* are important. If we think of them as just "monsters," we solidify our aversion and hatred toward them, which are really just parts of our own mind. If we think of them as just "beautiful," however, we are denying the destructive potential they have and the suffering they can cause. It's important to understand that they are both monsters and they have beauty.

The beautiful monsters have two types of beauty: The first is by their very nature. No matter how monstrous an emotion might seem, its deep, underlying nature is very different. Like the raw material of full-color 3D images projected on a screen is pure light, so the underlying raw material of our beautiful monsters is openness, clarity, and energy. So, beautiful monsters have that beauty. The second is that beautiful monsters seem ugly at first, but when we heal one, it becomes beautiful.

When we heal something, we understand that dynamic not just within ourselves but also within everyone who shares that wound. Many great beings have healed something and then become very wise and helped many people. If you have ten beautiful monsters, and another person has two, and you both heal them, who has more capacity? You with your ten beautiful monsters! You will have much greater understanding and capacity to help. But many people don't heal; they just live their whole life and suffer with their beautiful monsters.

Beautiful monsters are formed in various ways: sometimes we develop habits because of challenging relationships; sometimes tendencies get provoked by circumstances; sometimes repeated stress just makes us develop reactive habits. Something that was once helpful, like protecting ourselves in an unsafe environment, can become a beautiful monster when it gets hardened and habitual. We hate a certain kind of person or situation even though we are no longer in danger.

I often get asked, are all feelings and emotions beautiful monsters? I would say no. Normal anger is part of the healthy, authentic relative truth—there is healthy anger, healthy fear, healthy attachment. These are not beautiful monsters. Beautiful monsters form when there is some unhealthy distortion in our mind and feelings, and then we start to believe their version of relative truth. If we become caught up by these beautiful monsters they become our lenses, the way we see the world and see ourselves. When we heal those, we have normal, healthy emotions and experiences. Healthy human beings have a full range of emotions.

Beautiful monsters are like ice. Their nature is like water. We don't have to destroy the ice but melt it, free it into its natural state of flow. We all know ice is both beautiful and scary. It can be sharp and jagged and very destructive. It may be frozen, but it's not different from water. Beautiful monsters are like that. They are "frozen" patterns of reacting and resisting. We are looking for water but have ice instead. Then we forget what and try to get rid of the ice, or run away from the ice, and find water—peace and flow—somewhere else. So the question becomes, how to melt the ice? The warmth of our kindness toward our beautiful monsters, in the form of nonjudging—this allows the ice to start melting.

The Method

Please note: If you've had a history of trauma, these practices of radical nonresistance can be intense. Please use your common sense about how much you can reasonably take. Try this practice for very short periods of time, and use a base camp, a safe place to return to in between feeling the feelings directly. This handshake practice is for healing, not retraumatization. Consult with a mental health professional for support if that's helpful.

Handshake: Working with Our Beautiful Monsters

How do we face our beautiful monsters with friendliness rather than fear? Based on some traditional meditation techniques and my understanding of psychological wounding and healing, I developed what I call *handshake practice*. It is not a method as we normally think. It is more an attitude and a way of being. The handshake is between our awareness and our feelings. It is a metaphor for the stance we take, for how we can meet our beautiful monsters. Our minds have been pushing away or holding down our feelings and emotions for a long time. Now we are just extending our hand. Not running away, not fighting, just meeting. Essentially, handshake practice is to be fully aware of whatever is in you, especially feelings. If they have a story to tell, we just listen. I feel this practice of handshake is very important for these modern times, and has the potential to deeply heal us.

This kind of healing can best occur where our awareness touches our feelings. To heal, we need to feel our emotions in a raw and direct way. Then the wounds and patterns of resistance can start to open up from within. Otherwise we can try all sorts of healing techniques, but they may not really open us up. To actually transform, we need to make friends with our emotions.

Understanding the theory behind the handshake helps us because we can see why we need to work on our distorted beliefs and attitudes in order to have real transformation. Otherwise we can have temporary relief, but we will still be operating under the same assumptions and beliefs (for example, *I am not worthy*; *It is shameful to be angry*; *If I feel the fear, it will dominate me and I'll fall apart*). But just reading about and contemplating these ideas won't change much. We need to face our beautiful monsters. Facing them means *feeling* them. Actual transformation happens mostly on the feeling level. When we learn to experience our beautiful monsters without resistance and reaction, we can actually befriend them. This is very loving, very kind to the beautiful monsters—nonjudging is the kindness.

Handshake means being fully with the feeling. It is a very simple method to describe, but difficult to actually do for several reasons. First of all, our attitude is often that these beautiful monsters are just monsters and we want to fix them, to get rid of them. With that as a hidden agenda, handshake doesn't work. Handshake is not fixing but rather meeting and being.

TRY THIS: Sit for a few minutes, settling into a quiet, contemplative inner space. Consider the relationship between your mind and your emotional world. How does it feel? Is it loving and open? Is it strained or critical? Does your feeling world seem mostly numb or raw and dynamic? However you feel, be with it and relax for a while.

Then imagine if what you fear within yourself, your criticism, your doubt, your pride, became your friend. Imagine not being afraid of your feelings and emotions.

Another reason being with our feelings can be hard is that we can be a little afraid of our raw feelings and emotions. This is normal. But this is also why we need some courage to handshake our feelings. We have to be willing to feel our suffering, willing to take some hits. Think of a loving adult trying to hold a young child in a tantrum. The child screams and kicks and punches, and each time we gently put our hand on them, they push it away. But we understand they are upset and fundamentally beautiful and lovable, even in their contorted state. We keep offering our hand, even while they keep hitting it back. Eventually, they calm down and accept the open touch of love. The process of handshaking our beautiful monsters can be similar. Underneath, the beautiful monsters want to be friends, and they want to be free.

TRY THIS: Imagine a child who is upset and flailing. Imagine having deep love for the child and willingness to care even when being hit back for a little while. Then imagine offering that same attitude toward yourself, your own beautiful monsters.

Obstacles to Handshake

There are four main obstacles to handshaking; *suppressing*, *ignoring*, *indulging*, and *antidoting*. These are strong mental habits, probably the main ways we relate to our feelings and emotions. It's important to understand that handshaking is none of these.

Most of us are quite skilled at *suppressing*. An uncomfortable feeling or emotion pops up at an inconvenient time, and we push it right back down or stuff it under the carpet. This might work for a little while, but suppressing bleeds our energy, and the feeling or emotion will find a way to pop back up. For example, we might have a beautiful monster of self-doubt or unworthiness. When those feelings come up, we don't allow them, we don't listen to them, but rather we automatically judge them as painful and unacceptable and push them down, back into our subconscious.

Ignoring is another strategy we are highly familiar with. We simply run away, which means distracting ourselves. Where do we run? We can have positive distractions, like some spiritual activity, a train of thought, or maybe we just watch movies. The problem is that in the long run, ignoring our beautiful monsters does not help them heal. If we ignore them we might assume they are gone, but they're not. Ignoring feelings of unworthiness and losing ourselves in a TV show doesn't process or deal with the feelings; it's just a temporary Band-Aid.

Indulging is another way we often react. Handshaking, where we don't try to resist or fix the beautiful monster, can seem quite similar to indulging, but it's different. Handshaking meets and stays with the beautiful monster, while indulging believes its story, follows it, and lets it dominate us. Indulging in feelings of self-doubt would be sinking into a mood of insecurity and allowing the familiar narratives of self-doubt to dominate the mind.

Finally, there is *antidoting*, which is applying some method or commentary or sensemaking to fix a problem. It sounds good on the surface: We have a problem or a harmful habit, so we try to fix it, just like we fix our car or our bike when it's broken. Antidoting is like applying a remedy to a poison, putting a neutralizing emotion or thought onto the feeling of unworthiness to make it go away. Handshaking is feeling the feeling directly, without trying to make it go away. Another example of antidoting is telling myself that everything is fine when I actually feel that things are not okay. Handshaking is feeling the sense of not-okayness and making friends with it. Antidoting includes all sorts of psychological and spiritual approaches. But handshake is not an antidote. We're not trying to fix; we're just meeting and being, making friends with our beautiful monsters.

Antidoting is a *near enemy* of handshaking, because it is so easy to confuse the two. A *far enemy* is an obvious one, the enemy we can see facing us. A near enemy is sneaky; it is disguised as a friend, so close we often can't see it, or we don't know it's an enemy. Antidoting is like that. Say we've tried many other approaches for our self-doubt and they didn't work, and then we hear about handshake. We might think, *Oh, this sounds good; this is a subtle and gentle technique. I will handshake my beautiful monsters and they will dissolve or go away!* If we have this attitude, we have slipped into antidoting, which subtly sabotages our handshake.

Once we've met the feelings, and really felt them, we can just be with them. At first, don't talk, just be there. Once we can be with them, a shift will occur, and our feelings and beautiful monsters will start to trust us, little by little. The trust will develop because we are no longer suppressing or ignoring them. When they attack us, we just touch them—we aren't hitting back. The handshake has contact with open love. When they tell us their stories, we listen. They will start to open up and eventually will ask a question.

Then we can finally have a conversation. We can share our wisdom, giving good reasoning. We can tell them, *It's real, but it's not true*. The feeling is real, but the message is not true. *Yes, you really felt unworthy, but you aren't unworthy*. The mind can send a message to the feelings, because we've earned their trust. The feelings can communicate to the beautiful monsters. When the beautiful monster starts to understand and feel—*I am not a monster*—healing can happen. Until we touch the beautiful monster with awareness, with the kindness of nonjudging, the beautiful monster doesn't care what we say. We've been talking at it that way forever, and it hasn't helped. So what is different now? Instead of lecturing, we begin by simply being with the raw feeling of the beautiful monster. That is kindness.

If the emotional center of the beautiful monster transforms, that's the best. If not, first the surrounding feelings can transform, and then eventually the central feeling will transform. In our feeling world, okayness and not-okayness can exist at the same time. The best is if the not-okayness itself transforms into okayness. But sometimes, a little corner of your heart can feel not okay, while the other parts are okay. So then what do you do? You acknowledge the okay parts, but you still care for the not-okay part too.

Beautiful monsters have the ability to self-liberate; they have their own wisdom. Then what are we doing? Simply not disturbing them, and not leading them in the wrong direction, but allowing their own nature to shine. When we aren't suppressing, ignoring, or trying to fix them, then we are respecting them. Then liberation can happen. This point is a little tricky: If we know too much about this self-liberation, we can carry expectations. Expectations can sabotage our open, welcoming attitude and therefore sabotage our handshake. Wanting to change a beautiful monster is actually a beautiful monster in and of itself.

When you have the thought *Handshake is just providing the beautiful monster the opportunity to open up*, catch that thought and handshake that. If you do that a few times, those expectations will not continue.

The Four Steps in Handshake

Handshake lets our awareness be with whatever is happening in our feeling world without judgment, without resistance. Handshake practice can be broken into four steps: *meeting*, *being*, *waiting*, and *communicating*. The preparation for handshake practice is dropping, which we learned in chapter 2. But not all things can just be dropped: there are deeper, sticky issues that require more attention, more being with, more waiting, more love. We have become quite expert at avoiding, suppressing, indulging, and antidoting. These are hard habits to break. There can be many layers of fear, judgment, reactivity, and resistance between our awareness and our raw feelings. The practice of handshake is the way to navigate through this. We are learning to walk with dignity through the main door of our inner world, instead of squirming and sneaking around.

When mountaineers tackle a huge peak like Mount Everest they establish a base of operations for their climb, a place where they can return as needed to recover more strength for the ascent. Your personal base camp gives you a calm space away from raw emotions, a safe space to retreat to when the intensity is too much. The base camp can be a point of mindfulness, like neutral body sensations (the palms and feet can be good for this), following the breath, or the gentle breathing practice from chapter 3. You can use it as needed from time to time as part of the handshake practice.

Preparation: Dropping

◆ · · ◆ · · ◆

Begin by taking a relaxed posture as before—relaxed but with the spine straight, whether sitting or lying down. Spend a few minutes dropping the thinking mind and grounding awareness in the body. If it's useful, use the method from chapter 2 of lifting your hands into the air and letting gravity bring them down on the thighs with a good slap, along with a big breath out. Three things happen together; the thinking mind drops, the hands drop on the thighs, and you let out a deep breath. Then just rest there, in the body, with no agenda.

Don't look for any special state or special sensation. Just connect with what's there, the experience of the body in the present. Warm or cool, pleasant or unpleasant, tight or relaxed, tingling or numb—however it feels is fine. Rest there for a little while and then repeat several times, until you feel somewhat grounded in the body. As your awareness pervades your physical body, just be with the body sensations, however they are. Maybe an agenda has popped up, like you want to have a special, particular experience you want to avoid something. Keep gently letting go of any agendas. This allows what naturally wants to emerge to come into your awareness.

Step #1: Meeting

Now allow awareness to gently pervade the feeling world. Open awareness to moods, feelings, and emotions. Don't hold any goal, any aim. Just meet whatever feelings and emotions are there. Don't look for anything special, pleasant, or sublime, just be with what is arising. If you feel lousy, be with that. If you feel anxious, be with that feeling. If you feel angry or tense or tired, be with those feelings, and relax into them. If you feel great, peaceful, and relaxed, just be with that too. If you can't feel anything, just be with the numbness, or be with the peace.

◆

Feelings and emotions come and go on their own time; we don't have to look for them. They are always changing, pleasant to unpleasant to pleasant again. Rather than wrestling with each changing feeling, we are just meeting them and allowing whatever comes without an agenda. Keep connecting to the feeling world with this open, welcoming attitude. Whenever an agenda arises to get rid of something, or hold on to something, gently acknowledge it and be with that. Whatever the obstacle or criticism is, just be aware of it and be with that. You are the host of a banquet, standing at the door and meeting any of your feelings that show up. If something deeper and more intense shows up, it might be a beautiful monster. That's fine too.

This meeting practice is to extend your hand and say hello. Initially, we just allow thoughts to come and go, and try to stay with our feelings and emotions, but later we extend the handshake practice to encompass everything, including narratives and inner voices.

Step #2: Being

Stop looking away. Stop hiding. Turn toward it. Touch it. Feel it. Listen to it. As you adopt this attitude, you are allowing raw feelings to emerge. There is nothing special to do except be with them.

Don't suppress, don't avoid, don't indulge, and don't apply an antidote. We have been doing those things for far too long. It hasn't helped much. It hasn't gotten us a healthy relationship with our feelings. So let's try something different. Just being. Being is not fixing. We tend to think "being" means being *with* something. But you can also just be, without an object. Just be with being itself. Slowly we can learn to just be with the experiencer, without a particular object, naturally being in being itself. Just be, and as thoughts and emotions continue to arise and move, stillness of being remains too.

Over time, the hand doesn't need an object to hold, the hand itself becomes the resting, the stillness. If this experience organically develops out of handshake, this is a good sign. Handshake is an intimate way of being. It's different from an observer, which is safer and more distant. When the beautiful monsters come, this type of distant observing won't help so much. It doesn't touch the feeling world in the same way as handshake. Just be with whatever raw material arises without judging, and relax.

If a wild, deluded feeling shows up at your banquet—*I want to smash everything!*—just give your hand. The beautiful monster isn't giving its hand. But you are being kind and just being there. Even if the beautiful monster gives you a slap or a punch, it's okay. Take it. Be willing to suffer. This aggressiveness results from our suppressing them for a long time. Have a courageous attitude: *Okay, I am willing to suffer*. And if you find yourself judging, take a step back and handshake the judgment. If you notice an agenda, like wanting the emotion to go away, handshake that agenda. If you notice an aversion to the emotion, or an impatience, handshake that. Keep handshaking whatever comes up.

Take a radical approach: Be fully present with your feelings and emotions, without resistance. It's almost surrendering, trusting the innate wisdom of the emotions. This is a big step. It takes some guts, some courage. Feeling something we've been avoiding is not easy. This can be very intense. Jumping into the unknown water can be scary. When the time is right, though, you have to take the step. If you feel like you're holding back, if you feel like you're resisting, give the beautiful monster your hand.

It almost seems like indulging, but it is not indulging. If the emotion says *I can't take it*, you don't have to believe it, just feel it. If the feeling says *I want to destroy that*, just feel that emotion, but don't follow its orders. Allow awareness to feel the feeling fully, without resistance, without judgment. This is the practice of being.

Step #3: Waiting

Continue to practice being; give it some time. Don't rush into anything. There is nothing to accomplish. You are making friends, and it takes time. Once you can be, just keep being and wait. Waiting is also kindness, compassion. Practice patience. Here patience doesn't mean an agenda like, *I'll be patient with you until you go away and leave me alone.* Such an agenda can sidetrack the practice. Here patience means: *You can stay as long as you want. I don't care anymore whether you stay or go. We're friends now.*

This stage of waiting allows you to refine your handshake and make sure you are not rushing to make something happen, in which case our handshake is being sabotaged by antidoting. Or you might be rushing to lecture your beautiful monsters, before they trust you and are ready to listen. Just wait and relax.

There is a special relief when you actually drop in and just feel the feelings. You're being true to yourself. Suppressing and avoiding can make you feel emotionally ungrounded, like you're not centered in your feeling world. To drop in and feel, without judging, is a gift. It's like crying when your heart wants to release sadness, or taking a nap when you're exhausted, or eating a nourishing meal when you're feeling depleted and hungry. It's like asking for a hug when you feel bruised, and receiving a warm, solid embrace of total support. We can give ourselves that kind of relief and support, but we have to turn toward the pain, not away from it.

Step #4: Communicating

Talking to Your Beautiful Monsters

Once you are able to just be with your beautiful monsters, they may start to warm up, to open up. Actually they want to be friends. They want to be free. They may even ask a question. Then you can actually communicate. We gently tell them, *It's real, but not true. Your feeling is real. Your pain is real. But your narrative is not true.* And they will listen.

As you feel your agendas to fix something, or to make something dissolve or disappear, have fallen away, you may notice a shift. Something magical and unexpected happens when we stop trying to fix the beautiful monsters, when we stop trying to make them go away. The raw emotions, the stuckness, the numbness, are not as scary as they seem.

This is when true healing occurs. Now you've developed a healthy relationship between your mind and your feelings, and all sorts of communication can happen, both ways. You can share your wisdom and understanding. From their side, beautiful monsters carry their own wisdom and we can learn from them also.

The experience of handshaking self-doubt, for example, can teach us about the subconscious fear of success and flourishing, and teach us great compassion for others who share this beautiful monster. Once we make friends with our beautiful monsters, then we are no longer afraid of ourselves.

DANIEL GOLEMAN: THE SCIENCE

When Dr. Aaron Beck founded cognitive therapy, he shifted the therapeutic focus to the distorted ways people interpret their lives. My wife, Tara Bennett-Goleman, is a psychotherapist who had a major influence on integrating mindfulness with cognitive therapy, and, as Tsoknyi Rinpoche mentioned, then shared those insights with him—and he incorporated this approach to the mind in his idea of beautiful monsters.

Tara had been attending a series of intensive insight-meditation retreats during a period she was also engaged in a postgraduate training with Jeffrey Young, a protégé of Dr. Beck. While Beck's cognitive therapy in those days focused on helping people with depression and anxiety trouble, Young developed what he called *schema therapy*, a more psychodynamic approach to cognitive therapy that spotlighted common but troubling emotional patterns, like a sense of emotional deprivation or a fear of abandonment, that led to distorted thinking and emotional overreactions.

When Tara studied with him, Young was developing his model of what he called *schemas*, emotional patterns that we learn early in life and which plague our later relationships and cause us to suffer the same way over and over. Young put together insights, not just from cognitive therapy but also from gestalt therapy and attachment theory, into his schema therapy approach. A schema entails a set of beliefs about oneself and the world, and the linked emotions. When this packet of thoughts and feelings gets triggered we act in self-defeating ways. For instance, the "abandonment" schema triggers whenever a person feels someone significant to them does not value them and so will abandon them, putting them awash in sadness and feeling panicky. To protect against that panic, the person can either cling to their partner or cut off the relationship in a preemptive move.

Tsoknyi Rinpoche has visited with us often over the years. He was particularly intrigued by a clinical perspective on emotions and held intensive conversations with Tara, whom Beck called "a pioneer" in integrating mindfulness with cognitive therapy in her book *Emotional Alchemy: How the Mind Can Heal the Heart* (in fact, Tara taught mindfulness to Dr. Beck and his wife, a judge; at the time he had never heard of the method).

Tara's therapy work involved distressing emotions in general (and schema patterns when relevant). Her integration of Eastern and Western psychological perspectives saw each as a path to seeing ourselves and each other more clearly and compassionately, with a transformative, insightful awareness that leads to wise choices. Tara reviewed this new approach to emotional habits for Rinpoche, and these conversations fed into Rinpoche's notion of beautiful monsters and handshake practice. Here's how Tara recalls a few of those encounters:

In one of our dialogues about psychology, dharma, and science, I was telling Tsoknyi Rinpoche about the emotional patterns that I had seen in my therapy clients. Perhaps because he had been steeped in traditional Buddhist teachings, though he wanted to learn more, he was concerned that recognizing them might lead people to reify these patterns more strongly. I assured him that actually it could have the opposite effect— that acknowledging one's own or another's patterns can help us not to take it so personally. You see it more as the pattern, not the person, enhancing their confidence rather than their ego and increasing their understanding and compassion.

I can't say that this perspective represents how Western psychotherapy views psychological patterns. But since I have had a foot in both the worlds of Western psychology and Buddhist psychology, it's how I see them.

I told him how I use a scene from The Wizard of Oz *as a metaphor that illustrates this perspective. In the scene, Dorothy and her companions get to Oz's castle, and as they walk into Oz's room they suddenly see a huge moving image of a face on the screen with a booming voice, "I AM OZ!"*

They're startled and back away. But then Dorothy's little dog, Toto, runs over to a booth and pulls back the curtain. Inside, a little old man is stooped over the controls, using special effects to create that overpowering voice via a loudspeaker. He says, "Pay no attention to that man behind the curtain!"

As they confront him he comes out of his booth and becomes his genuine self. No longer so scary, he apologizes and starts to help them—including helping Dorothy get back home to Kansas.

This is how these emotional patterns work. They bellow loud, sometimes scary messages, and we think of them as real. But an honest introspection acts like an inner Toto that pulls back the curtain, allowing us to see them as they are. They become more and more transparent and eventually lose their power.

Cognitive therapy aims to change distorted emotional patterns to more adaptive ones. Tara added mindfulness to this work. In Tara's work, clarifying distortions via mindfulness lets us see these patterns more clearly, as they actually are. At the heart of each of these emotional habits lies an unsettling feeling, and a schema's distorted coping mechanism can deprive us of a richer life and a reparative relationship.

In *Emotional Alchemy* Tara described ten of these emotional patterns (and later developed more in her book *Mind Whispering: A New Map to Freedom from Self-Defeating Emotional Habits*) and explained them to Rinpoche, who said this might help him better understand his Western students. Rinpoche's talent for memorizing (perhaps from his training as a Buddhist scholar) paid off in how readily he grasped the emotional alchemy system, as he was developing his own. Among this set of ten is *vulnerability to harm*, as Young called it. This schema can be felt as mild uneasiness, but at its extreme becomes intense fears like agoraphobia, where someone dreads leaving their house for fear they will be severely injured or die. In short, the person seizes on a potential (though extremely unlikely) possibility and catastrophizes—escalating a normal fear out of control while ignoring the low risk likelihood, and imagining with certainty the awful things that could happen. The result: panic and paralysis. That's the cost. The emotional payoff: not having to face the dreaded even deeper terror that hides behind the vulnerability pattern.

Tara tells of a woman whose father nearly died of a heart attack when she was fourteen, and who told her, "You're the only reason I'm trying to live." She developed a fear that his very life depended on her. She became a health care worker—and a chronically worried one. She was true to the emotional pattern of seizing on a small something, only slightly worrisome, and blowing it up into a full-fledged catastrophe in her mind. So if her boyfriend mentioned he had mild heartburn she'd worry he was really having a heart attack.

The common roots roots of this chronic worry are growing up with a parent who had the same tendency. In adulthood the anxiety can focus anywhere from economic insecurity to health or the safety of people one cares about. This intense worry differs from the adaptive kind, where concern leads us to prepare for an actual risk. But, Tara notes in *Emotional Alchemy*, the problem comes when anxiety is exaggerated out of proportion.

She observes that one road to healing for this pattern can be mindful awareness of the thoughts and feelings that lead to panic, investigating exaggerated fears and training the mind to see these feelings and the situation that triggered them more clearly. Mindfully monitoring your anxious thoughts lets you choose not to let them drive what you do—the beginning of emotional freedom. Some of this direct, nonreactive, mindful presence with such deep feelings can be seen in Tsoknyi Rinpoche's handshake method.

One of the variations of the vulnerability-to-harm pattern is social anxiety, where someone fears being judged harshly or otherwise put down. People with this psychological problem are not only terrified of, say, giving a speech in public, but also dread situations like meeting strangers or simply being judged negatively by others. So they twist their lives to avoid social situations where they might feel socially anxious.

Volunteers with social anxiety were studied in the neuroscience lab of Philippe Goldin at the University of California, Davis. Goldin has a unique perspective on studying the mind and brain: Before going into clinical psychology and neuroscience as a postgraduate fellow at Stanford, he spent six years in Nepal and Dharamshala, India, studying Tibetan Buddhist philosophy and practices. He has done one of the few scientific studies of the ways an inner stance of acceptance impacts how we react to our upsetting emotional habits.

Goldin recruited volunteers who suffered from social anxiety and had them recall a disturbing incident—an actual situation—where they felt acute anxiety. Then they would write down in their own words exactly what happened and what negative thoughts about themselves went through their heads during the upsetting event. Among the more common thoughts: "Other people could see how anxious I was," "People always judge me," and "I am ashamed of my shyness."

Each of these thoughts triggers a cascade of negative feelings. In the brain such thoughts themselves trigger the neural alarm circuitry for anxiety. Goldin's team used those negative thoughts as triggers during a brain scan and saw that circuitry light up as it went into action.

Goldin went a step further. He trained one group of volunteers with social anxiety to simply observe their thoughts and feelings, just noticing them rather than reacting to them. He instructed them, "Just trust in allowing your moment-to-moment experience. Watch it like a stream flowing by, without acting on those thoughts or feelings in any way."

Researchers use the term *acceptance* for this nonreactive stance toward our troubling emotions. Chris Gerner, a psychotherapist, views acceptance as a major part of having compassion for ourselves. He sees several steps in this process, which seem to parallel Rinpoche's handshake practice. It starts with resistance, the common tendency to avoid uncomfortable feelings. But in the next step we turn toward our own discomfort with interest. As we manage to stay with those feelings, we begin to feel okay with the discomfort and become able to let them come and go without having to react. Finally comes what Rinpoche calls the handshake, where we make friends with the once upsetting feelings.

Brain researchers—Goldin among them—find that the triggering thoughts and feelings activate extensive circuitry for alarm, including the amygdala. But research led by Hedy Kober at Yale shows that the inner stance of accepting our feelings lessens the amygdala reactivity, making it easier to simply tune into upsetting emotions without having them drive what we think or do. Acceptance, she found, also made physical pain easier to bear. The title of her article on these findings: "Let It Be." Turns out to be good advice.

Philippe Goldin's research had a similar yield. He found that people with social anxiety who simply paid attention to their anxieties in an accepting, nonreactive way had their anxiety reduced. Perhaps surprisingly, their anxiety lessened—as did amygdala reactivity—as much as did that of a comparison group who handled their social anxiety with cognitive therapy, one of the nonpharmaceutical treatments of choice.

Cognitive therapy, where a person challenges their scary thoughts, among other tactics, produced an increase in activity in areas like the verbal cortex and other circuitry that such mental activity involves. Yet while the acceptance approach activated none of this circuitry, both interventions yielded similar reductions in the person's anxiety.

As Goldin explained, "Acceptance loosens the tendrils that grasp on to the loaded thoughts."

"Leave your front door and back door open. Let thoughts come and go. Just don't serve them tea."

FIVE

. —— . ✦ . —— .

ESSENCE LOVE

TSOKNYI RINPOCHE: THE EXPLANATION

Several years ago I was traveling and teaching a lot and had become a little disconnected. Outwardly I was fine and could perform my duties, but inwardly I felt a sort of hollowness. I was in a hotel room in New Delhi during a long series of travels and was just sitting lazily on my bed, flipping through channels on the TV.

Suddenly my attention was caught by a TV image of a handsome man and a beautiful woman wearing elegant, flowing clothes, walking together with poise and confidence down a country lane. Their clothes and her long hair were swaying in a gentle breeze. The man's shirt was untucked and partially unbuttoned, and you could glimpse four of his six-pack. The other two were hidden under his pants, but you knew they were there. I reached down to my own belly and felt my one-pack.

The couple seemed so effortlessly happy and confident, which I didn't feel in myself. I wanted what they had. Under one of their arms was a sleek silver laptop—it was an advertisement for a Sony Vaio computer.

I shook my head and thought, *This is ridiculous; this is just an ad, and they are just actors.* I knew how many takes a film crew can need to get the perfect shot. I knew they were professional models and actors trained to convey a particular emotion and mood, designed to influence and persuade the watcher to feel a certain way. I changed the channel and forgot about it.

But then a few weeks later I was in Singapore and I saw the same ad, and again it caught me for a few moments. The wind was blowing her hair into his face, but he didn't care, because he was so happy, so cool. Again, I shook my head and forgot about it.

A few weeks later I was in Paris, traveling and teaching, and I saw the two models on a massive billboard, holding the laptop and looking very chic. My gaze moved on to something else.

But after seeing that billboard in Paris I arrived in New York, and I bought that Sony Vaio computer.

For two weeks I was quite excited about this new possession. It boosted my mood, and I kind of forgot about the hollowness. I was having fun playing with it and admiring its elegant design. I felt quite modern and cool taking it to a coffee shop with me.

But after a few weeks the effect was wearing off. I started

to notice my greasy fingerprints all over the screen. They hadn't mentioned that in the ad.

Then I was back in Europe for some more work and the plug didn't fit the outlets. I had to get a bunch of plug adapters. This also wasn't mentioned in the ad.

Several weeks later I traveled to the high plateau of Tibet and the computer crashed. Apparently, the bumpy roads, dust, and altitude were too much for it. They also didn't mention this in the advertisement.

A Well-Being Independent of Circumstance

Through the handshake practice—meeting our feeling world in a raw, direct way with no agenda—we may glimpse from time to time a natural well-being not dependent on our circumstances. As we make friends with our beautiful monsters, emotions, feelings, moods, reactions, and resistances, we start to heal ourselves deeply and organically. The outcome of this process is the increasing availability of a basic okayness underlying the feeling world. I like to call this *essence love*.

It's not loud and flashy—it doesn't come announced by trumpets and fireworks. It's quiet and subtle. We are just okay for no particular reason. It's like a subtle inner warmth, underneath the shifting feelings, emotions, and moods. We can call it "the true home of the feeling world." From a Tibetan Buddhist perspective, this is the quality of *bindu*, seeds of energy, and part of the subtle body, which differs from our physical body. We are born with it. Healthy children feel it as an inner joy, a spark of life, a playfulness, a readiness to give and receive love.

As we grow up in the modern world and participate in stressful and competitive schooling, socializing, and work, our intrinsic essence love can get covered up by layers of stress, self-judgment, hope, and fear. Although this inner spark can be almost completely obscured (for example, in cases of depression, burnout, and anxiety disorders), it is never actually destroyed or lost. We often just can't find it, connect to it, and experience it.

Through handshake practice we can begin to reconnect with this essence love that resides within us. The more we connect with and nurture our essence love, the more we can feel its qualities—that basic sense of okayness, and its signs: unconditional well-being; a readiness to love; a spark of joy, clarity, courage, and humor.

Essence love is subtle, not loud or dramatic. It's like a quiet whisper in the background of our feeling world, softly saying, "I'm okay. I don't know why, but I'm okay." We can easily miss it, because we are accustomed to looking for louder, more colorful things—like emotions, pain, and pleasure. Essence love is much more subtle than excitement about a new experience, possession, or relationship.

Love's Essence and Love's Expression

There's an important distinction between what I call *essence love* and *expression love*. *Expression love* is directed outwardly—it includes parental love, romantic love, friendship love, devotional love, loving kindness, and so on. These are all wonderful and valuable for a healthy life, but here I am drawing attention to something more fundamental, one step back: the raw stuff from which our expressions of love emerge—essence love.

This is where love is born; it's the readiness to give and receive love. When radiating from essence love, expression love can be healthy. I believe connecting to and nurturing essence love is an important way to improve not only our own happiness within ourselves but also to improve the quality of our relationships.

We need to distinguish essence love from self-love. To me, self-love sounds like a form of expression love directed back at ourself, like a flashlight pointed back at the person holding it. This sounds like it could be very healthy, like a soothing balm— an antidote to self-judgment, self-recrimination, and self-hatred. Certainly, feeling good about ourselves is much better than harshly judging ourselves.

The spiritual and secular worlds seem to be full of teachings on the importance of self-love. I suspect there are a variety of meanings given to the idea of loving ourselves, and some may overlap with what I'm trying to say here.

The quality of essence love is a little different though. It is directionless, like a natural field of unconditional well-being within our feeling world. It isn't focused on anyone, even ourselves. Essence love is not the mind generating a positive thought or feeling about our sense of self, or about an image of our body. We aren't generating it and directing it anywhere. Essence love is already there inside us, from birth. We can notice it and nurture it, and then it can overflow from within. Connecting to essence love isn't exactly an antidote to self-judgment but rather heals a sense of inner hollowness.

The Opposite of Essence Love Is Hollowness

Let's return to that ad for the Sony Vaio. All that travel had led me to be flipping through TV channels until I landed on that seductive ad. Inside, my essence love was blocked somehow. When we cannot connect to our intrinsic essence love, we can feel a sense of hollowness inside.

When we connect with our intrinsic essence love, the hollowness dissolves into well-being, a subtle warmth. Then our expressed love can be much less conditional, because we are coming from a healthier place of okayness deep within ourselves.

When we cannot connect to essence love, instead of okayness, we can feel something deep in our being is not okay. Instead of well-being, we feel we are emotionally imbalanced and hungry. We want to fill this hollowness underlying our feeling world. Consciously or not, a lot of our behavior can be motivated by this desire, like a secret agenda operating in our lives. We try to fill the hollowness by consuming things, possessing things, and having gratifying experiences one after another—as happened to me with that Sony Vaio laptop.

Inner hollowness plus modern consumer culture is a dangerous combination. Advertisers are smart and target the hollowness with false promises, triggering a continuous cycle of hope and fear. "Feeling empty inside? If you buy this, you will be happy. If you don't have this, you'll continue to feel bad." If we are disconnected from essence love, we can subconsciously internalize these messages, and our consumption can become compulsive. In extreme cases, we can become trapped in downward spirals, addicted to self-destructive substances and behaviors.

Our relationships, too, can be tainted by a secret agenda to fill the hollowness. With hollowness instead of essence love, our expression of love can be motivated in part by a sense of lacking, a desire to fill the hollowness. Then how we express our love can become quite conditional. It may not be explicit; we may not even be fully aware of it. Practically, however, our behavior can convey a condition, *I will offer my love if you perform x, y, and z for me, and I don't have to feel that hollowness.* This secret agenda can compromise, even sabotage, our ability to have healthy relationships and offer unconditional love.

It is particularly important for children to feel a background of unconditional love. Even though there may be surface-level conditions, such as getting scolded when they misbehave or their grades drop, or rewarded if they perform well, their healthy development depends on feeling a stable, strong sense of unconditional love underneath how they do or with any other behavior. Otherwise they can confuse their self-worth with how well they perform in class, arts, sports, and so on. Confusing self-worth with performance is a prime reason essence love gets covered up.

Essence Love: Unfavorable and Favorable Conditions

Earlier we discussed how the speed of the modern world can be challenging for keeping our energy grounded, balanced, and healthy. In a similar way, the modern world is full of hindrances to connecting with our natural well-being, posing challenges for essence love to flourish both during our school years and in our adult life. Such unfavorable conditions are unhealthy in that they can block or obscure essence love. They can even make essence love invisible, which means we are unable to feel and experience it.

As I've traveled around the world many times, I have noticed that as modern education and work culture spreads, essence love seems to be more and more difficult to see. One reason may be how busy we are. We are usually lost in our schedule—go do this, now do homework, now do that—from a fairly young age, in school and in other activities. This busyness brings an almost continuous involvement in hope and fear, feelings that block essence love. From a deeper perspective, all conditional love has some flavor of hope and fear, no matter what the specifics.

On the other hand there are many moments and situations that can trigger essence love. Making love, affection, deep devotion, deep love . . . these are among countless conditions that put us in touch with essence love. Others include beautiful music, being in nature, gentle long breathing in and out, nourishing the body with delicious, healthy food, and nourishing our *bindu* (seeds of energy in the "subtle body") with gentle yoga and healthy exercise.

Memories of unconditional love in your life can also be a powerful trigger. It may or may not be from an important relationship; it can even be of a casual moment. Maybe someone just lovingly gave you water when you were thirsty. Memories of kindness, of love received without condition, can help trigger essence love. Another common trigger are memories of natural beauty, of seeing flowers, for example, and of how you felt when you saw them. They weren't *your* flowers, you didn't own them—but they helped you anyway. Or maybe you went to the top of a hill and saw a beautiful sunset. The sunset is not essence love, just a very conducive moment for allowing innate okayness to freely come out.

There is some taste of freedom in that. Our challenge is once we experience those things to learn not to rely on them, whether the sunset or someone's flower garden. Instead, through our practice, we can come to experience essence love at any time, any moment, because we can come to trust that: *This is inside me; this is my nature.*

Still, those essence love connectors are a plus. I like to call them a bonus—and why not have a bonus? But at the same time, they are unreliable. Everything we experience is impermanent. Impermanent means some cause or condition might change the circumstance. You might have wonderful sex, but because of impermanence, and because other factors can intervene, next time you might not have fantastic sex, fantastic food, fantastic music, fantastic anything.

Next time you go to see a music performance, you might have a big quarrel with your partner, and that music might not give you the same pleasure. Any such factor can disrupt and change the experience at any time. So we have to learn acceptance, we have to learn change, we have to learn to let go. We have to find our essence love without depending on so many conditions. Actually, essence love does not depend on any such conditions.

The more we depend on external circumstances to connect with essence love, the weaker and weaker we become. Our brain loses interest in repetitiousness, tunes out what was once an essence love trigger, and so we become lazy. Even hearing something true and helpful, we might feel bored, jaded, and aloof—"Oh, I heard that before. . . ." One day we may find we have lost our resource; our triggers have lost their potency. For example, let's say there are fifteen major circumstances that trigger essence love for us. It's not infinite. Food, sex, skiing, going to the mountains, and so on . . . we keep repeating these. But one day they no longer work. We have gotten used to them, habituated, and they don't bring excitement anymore.

Then we can lose hope, thinking, *Nothing can make me happy*. I call this phenomenon *high-class suffering*. We buy something new and we get excited for two weeks, like me with my Sony Vaio. We feel compelled to keep repeating that trigger in hopes of finding essence love again. If we eat our favorite food every day for a month, instead of essence love, we'll have nausea and vomiting. Inner development, on the other hand, doesn't have such an end. It doesn't decrease but keeps increasing.

Take, for example, what happened to me recently. I went to Pokhara, a famous mountainside area in Nepal, and it was wonderful. We stayed in a rustic place out of town, like camping.

There was no toilet, no shower; it barely had electricity. I suffered a little bit but enjoyed it a lot. Then when I came home, I saw everything as so comfy and convenient. My toilet is just two steps away. I have running water, hot water, and my bed is so comfortable. For a day I enjoyed all that comfort, but then I forgot about it. It just became normal again as I thought, *Of course it should be like this*. I took it for granted rather than appreciating it.

A problem arises, though, when we confuse the trigger, the condition, for the essence love, which is intrinsic. Conditions can inspire essence love, but any method—any doing something—cannot *create* essence love. In fact, although these activities may activate essence love, one day we will not need to depend on any of them. Instead, through our mind, through our practice, we will reconnect to essence love without needing those conditions.

That independence from externals marks the beginning of inner freedom. Then even in a dark room, by ourselves, we can connect to essence love. Even in the moment of dying, we will be able to connect with essence love.

The Practice

Not intense, like intoxicating bliss or pleasure, essence love is more like a subtle warmth or humidity in a room, which we may not notice because we're swept up by colorful objects or people in the room. Crucially, essence love is always present within us, and once we connect to it and nurture it, we can notice it underneath any feeling state, emotion, or mood. Here are some practices that can help you activate essence love.

Noticing

Take a relaxed posture sitting on the ground or in a chair. For a few moments, drop your thoughts and settle your awareness into your body. Now gently open your eyes and softly gaze into the room. Let your attention notice the objects in the room, as you normally would. Now release attention from those objects and just notice the space in the room for a little while. Now pay attention to the objects again. Then again let go of focusing on the objects and just notice the space that holds everything. Allow awareness to go back and forth, noticing what these two modes feel like.

Reflection on Craving

In my tradition we talk about "hungry ghosts," spirits with tiny throats and huge bellies, who wander around tormented by hunger and thirst, never feeling satisfied because nothing they consume can ever satiate their desires.

Hungry ghosts serve as a metaphor for various kinds of insatiable cravings, where we lose sight of the consequences of our actions, and get locked into a cycle of trying to satisfy cravings that just keep coming back. A traditional example of trying to satisfy such cravings is like drinking salty water.

Contemplating such experiences—whether as literal or metaphorical—can be a source of great compassion. And it can be sobering and helpful to sometimes reflect on how "hungry ghost mentality" operates in our own lives.

◆ · · ◆ · · ◆

Take a relaxed posture sitting on the ground or in a chair. For a few moments, drop the thinking mind and settle awareness into the body. Contemplate the existence of "hungry ghosts," beings driven by intense craving that can never be satiated. Contemplate if and how this mentality shows itself in your own mind, in your own life. Consider that nothing you can consume from outside will ever fully satisfy you or provide you with lasting well-being. Reflect that you already possess an intrinsic basic okayness, it's already inside of you, and it's a source of endless well-being. Aspire to reconnect and nurture your birthright of essence love.

◆

The Trigger Method

Triggers make use of conducive conditions and activities for activating essence love. We each have many possible triggers, inspirations, and associations, so these particular triggers will have different effects for each of us. Feel free to substitute a healthy trigger that works for you, like a memory of being loved unconditionally, or watching the sunset.

The main point here is to allow the trigger or inspiration to activate essence love, and then spend some time noticing the essence love itself, withdrawing attention from the trigger.

✦ · · ✦ · · ✦

Triggering essence love with music

Prepare the practice by queuing up a piece of music (or several tracks) that you find particularly beautiful, that really move you. Choose a length of music that is half to two-thirds as long as your practice session.

Take a comfortable, relaxed posture and begin by dropping awareness into the body for a few minutes. Then start playing your prepared music. Allow the music to wash over you, through you. Appreciate its beauty for a few minutes. Allow it to inspire you. Notice the sensations and feelings in your body while listening. Now try to connect to a more subtle underlying quality in the feeling world, the basic okayness or well-being. As the music ends, withdraw attention first from the music and then from the sensations and feelings in the body, and try to just be with the essence love, the okayness. No need to do anything with it, just be with it, immersed.

Triggering essence love with long, gentle breathing

Begin in the same way, by taking a comfortable, relaxed posture and dropping awareness into the body for a few minutes. Now start deliberate and gentle long breathing in and out for five to ten minutes. Settle into a relaxed rhythm. Allow the gentle breathing to relax you, nurture you, inspire you. Notice the subtle sensations in your body during the long in-and-out breaths, maybe tingling, maybe warmth, maybe peace, maybe a little joy or subtle bliss. Now withdraw attention from the breath and sensations and try to notice the subtle well-being, or okayness, underneath. When it feels right, allow breathing to return to normal and just remain with the essence love, allowing it to wash through your being. There is no need to do anything in particular, just reacquaint yourself with this inner okayness.

Triggering essence love with gentle movement

You can use any kind of gentle movement you prefer, such as qigong, gentle yoga, tai chi, stretching, walking, and so on. Begin by dropping into the body and being in the body for a few minutes. Now begin to move gently in whatever way you've chosen. Enjoy moving your body fluidly, or stretching, or walking. Be aware of your body's position in space and be as embodied as possible while you move. Allow the movement to inspire you. Now pay more attention to the sensations throughout your body. Finally, withdraw attention from the movement and sensations and try to notice the okayness, the basic well-being of essence love underneath the sensations. Just be with that. Whether you keep moving or come to rest, keep noticing and being with your intrinsic essence love. Reacquaint yourself and let it nurture you.

◆

The Natural Method

◆ · ◆ · ◆

Take a comfortable, relaxed posture and practice dropping awareness into the body and resting in the body for a few minutes. Bring to mind an experience of handshake practice when you opened up from within and a glimpse of essence love you may have had. Now try to directly experience natural well-being, the okayness, again. If you can find it, just be with that. You can use a tiny bit of mindfulness to help reconnect, being mindful of okayness. You can search a little bit for the view of okayness: "Where are you? Where is okayness?" You aren't looking for a conditional one. If you find some well-being, some spot of okayness in your feeling world, then maintain that. Be with that, with the help of gentle mindfulness.

If you cannot find that soft corner of okayness or well-being, then go back to handshake. Right there in that moment, whatever is in the moment of your experience—fear, sadness, or numbness—meet that and stay with that. When it opens, there is essence love again. Keep doing this, and one day essence love will be more available. As soon as you look for essence love, it will say, *Oh, I'm here*. At those times, you won't need to do handshake practice, you can just be with essence love and nurture that.

If you're not sure, or if instead of essence love you find hollowness, you can still keep looking. You can call out silently, in your mind, *Hey, essence love, where are you?* It might come out, because you've already experienced it before through handshake. You just have to look and search. Sometimes you have to shout to yourself, *Where are you?!* If it's available, wonderful. If not, handshake. That's why handshake practice is so important, all along. Any hindrances, blockages, at any point, have to open up. The way to open up is handshake.

◆

Essence love is not so much a practice as a basic well-being or okayness that we're born with. Some people have essence love readily available, because beautiful monsters haven't blocked it. They just have to turn attention to it, notice it. Others cannot find it, not because it has disappeared, but just because it's obscured. But these methods can help us reconnect to essence love.

Any time you have connected with essence love you can nurture it by just being with it, immersing in it. Rest in it. Bathe in it. Let it wash over you. Let it well up inside you. Notice its subtle qualities—okayness for no reason, a readiness to give and receive love, a spark of joy and humor, natural clarity, courage.

You may feel like expressing this love, joy, humor, or courage. That impulse is very positive, but there is no need to express anything just yet. While practicing, just keep connecting and being with essence love, strengthening the connection. You will have plenty of opportunities in daily life to express your essence love outwardly. Now is a time to strengthen your own access, your own trust in finding the home of the feeling world, your natural well-being. Just rest in your home.

A key point: recognize essence love as often as possible in formal meditation practice as well as daily life, with and without the use of triggers. Follow the pithy advice: "short moments, many times." This reminds us to get reacquainted, to strengthen the connection and nurture the essence love within.

I believe these ways to connect with essence love are key to a heathy human life endowed with well-being. Otherwise, we can be perpetually stuck depending on external conditions, always seeking self-gratification in something other than our own being. It's like we're always hungry, trying to eat something, to fill the hollowness. When our minds are like this, we never become free, and by "free" I mean really deep down, a carefree, cheerful happiness.

The great masters of the past generations had this cheerfulness deep down. Their minds were not judging, not comparing, but compassionate, free, full of well-being, and at the same time they also had concern and alertness. Essence love is crucial for all of this. My aspiration is that we discover this within ourselves and share it with others.

DANIEL GOLEMAN: THE SCIENCE

It had been a fruitful week for me at a retreat Tsoknyi Rinpoche taught. The practice sessions had left me in a state where I felt continuously at ease and "happy for no reason," as Rinpoche puts it. I was feeling replete just as I was, with no need for anything else. Everything felt just right, whatever happened.

Tara and I were driving Rinpoche from the retreat to our house, a few hours away, for a visit.

"I feel really, really, good," I told Rinpoche. "Now I know what 'well-being' means."

"You're in touch with okayness, the sign of essence love," Rinpoche replied.

"I'd like it to last forever," I said.

"It will last as long as you can continue to find this place within yourself," he told me.

But once back home I got caught up in the whirl of my daily to-do lists, calls, emails, and other must-dos, and that sense of well-being slowly faded away, covered over by the daily cascade of stuff to do, think about, worry over.

There are two kinds of happiness. The first, as Rinpoche points out, depends on what happens to us in the course of a day—and while it gives us "ups" when good things happen, we can take a dive into bad feelings if life does not go well. That emotional seesaw gradually wore away my retreat high.

The second kind of happiness, more steady, comes from within and stays with us no matter what occurs. That's what Tsoknyi Rinpoche calls *essence love*, with its telltale feeling of okayness, where we can be happy for no particular reason—that is, not depending on something outside ourselves to make us feel good. It's a steady, upbeat quality no matter what may be happening—even disappointments, frustrations, setbacks.

There's a sense in which psychological theory is autobiography—that is, psychologists intuit where to focus their research based, to some degree, on their own experience. That may be one reason the field has historically had little to say about an inner state that stays positive no matter what happens to us—psychologists themselves likely have been strangers to this experience. And so that kind of equanimity no matter what happens had been off the field's map of human experience. Psychology's focus, instead, had been to a great degree on pathological states like extreme anxiety and depression.

Psychological science has only recently begun to focus on qualities related to what Rinpoche calls *okayness*. This shift toward a more upbeat focus started with a surge of interest in the positive psychology movement, which brought into the science's gaze more upbeat aspects of our experience—awe, gratitude, and compassion among them.

This new focus highlighted qualities sharing elements with

essence love, such as "intrinsic happiness," or, borrowing a word from Greek, *eudomania*, sometimes translated as "flourishing." This variety of happiness comes from within and seems largely impervious to the events of our lives.

The closest parallel to okayness in psychology may be the new field of well-being, and the realization—and scientific verification—that this positive inner state can be cultivated: well-being is a skill. My old friend Richie Davidson (a student of Tsoknyi Rinpoche's brother Mingyur Rinpoche, and a well-known neuroscientist) leads a group at the University of Wisconsin who are promulgating well-being, both by doing research on the topic and by offering a free app to help people get there.

The key principle underlying this research sees that we are able to cultivate an inner sense of well-being. The general idea in brain science depends on "neuroplasticity," that the more we practice a given routine, the stronger the underlying brain circuitry becomes. This is the sense, as Davidson puts it, in which well-being is a skill we can practice and master. That goes for meditation practice just as it does for a golf swing.

"Short moments, many times" serves as a reminder to regularly practice these mental moves; they will then occur more often and more naturally. In fact the Tibetan word for meditation, *gom*, means something like "getting used to it." In other words, the more we can connect with our essence love, and so become more familiar with this sense of okayness, the more readily we can access it.

A key component of well-being, the Davidson group proposes, rests in the activity of a key region in the prefrontal cortex, the brain's executive center, located just above the eyes and behind the forehead. The brain circuitry converging in this region fosters self-awareness, in the sense of being better able to track our own thoughts and feelings, and notice when we are distracted—the key to bringing our focus back to what's going on right now.

Research at Harvard and elsewhere finds that the more our mind wanders, the worse we feel. So, for instance, the more time people spend doomscrolling on their mobile phones, the more likely they are to report being depressed. On the other hand, the Davidson group has found that being able to bring our attention to what's going on in and around us in the present predicts a stronger sense of well-being. This accords with findings from those who study positive psychology: the ability to be reflective about our experience helps us have happier moods.

Here an open curiosity about our emotional habits and the thoughts that go with them—as when we witness these come and go with acceptance, in the handshake practice—also contributes to our sense of well-being.

Critical brain circuits for this part of well-being center on the prefrontal cortex—for instance, becoming aware of our thoughts involves circuitry on the side region. Being able to manage our own emotional state hinges on a strong connectivity between circuitry in the prefrontal region that connects to the amygdala, the brain's radar for threat and a trigger for feelings like anger and fear.

Meditation of many types seems to facilitate this brain shift. When we look at our own mind with an attitude of acceptance (the heart of handshake practice), the benefits at the biological level appear even greater—as signified, for instance, by lessened biological signs of stress.

When I talked to Richie about well-being he directed me to research his group had done on resilience, the ability to recover quickly from being upset. Some people are by their nature slow to recover—but, as Richie points out, we can all learn to recover from upsets more readily.

Recovering quickly from the upsets and biological changes stress creates is one of three ways practicing methods like the handshake can help us. Another has to do with how easily we are triggered to get upset. Some people find their day full of upsetting, disturbing events, while others react little or not at all to those same disturbances. And this too can be improved with the right practice.

The third aspect of emotional reactivity resides in how intensely we experience our upsets. Again, for some people an emotional trigger creates a high level of distress and physiological upset, while for the less reactive folks among us an emotional trigger registers as a blip, not a thunderstorm.

As we've seen, the handshake offers a practical way to deal with our emotional triggers and the resulting upsets. And that method opens a doorway for our becoming more unflappable: that sense of okayness.

There are other pillars of well-being, Davidson's group finds. One comes from simple self-inquiry, examining our emotions and their causes with an attitude of acceptance rather than judgment. That method, of course, aligns with the "handshake" that yields okayness. Brain research suggests this process activates areas in the executive center (the same ones used for managing disturbing emotions) and a neural network that during such "constructive self-inquiry." The result: that sense of well-being.

Another pillar of well-being that's quite similar to the handshake practice is what's called *insight*, where we become aware of that voice in our head that's talking to us from the moment we wake up in the morning until we fall asleep. Sometimes that voice gives us a pep talk, leaving us feeling more energized and enthusiastic about life—that's a boost to our positive mood.

But that same voice can become judgmental, highly critical of what we do, say, or even think. In that case it helps to find a steady place in our mind where we can let those thoughts come and go. That's akin to what the handshake practice offers us. As those negative thoughts wane, our feelings of well-being blossom.

Having compassion toward ourselves and an accepting attitude, research finds, enhances our sense of well-being in ways ranging from being better able to handle disturbing feelings to better empathy skills, like picking up subtle social cues. In contrast, rigidity and self-judgment in how we view our thoughts and feelings sets us up for depression and anxiety.

In terms of brain activity, this aspect of a positive sense of well-being seems associated with strong connections between the executive centers in the prefrontal cortex and what's known as the "default mode network," a set of brain circuits that become more active when our minds are wandering, as in a daydream—a mental state where we are more prone to ruminate about upsetting thoughts over and over rather than think in more constructive ways.

The hallmark of essence love and the okayness we feel goes

beyond the lessened likelihood of emotional problems like depression and anxiety. It's the upside that makes the real difference in our inner state: the "spark" that goes along with feelings of joy and aliveness.

While these feelings of okayness brought by connecting with our essence love is, in a real sense, its own reward, there are a range of other pluses in our physical and emotional health. For one, those who report a higher level of well-being are more resilient to stress; they have a quicker recovery time when they get upset.

Along with this stress resilience come a host of other health benefits, including a lessened risk of heart disease and other medical disorders that are worsened by stress-caused inflammation. These include arthritis, diabetes, and asthma. Likewise, there's strong data saying well-being lessens our vulnerability to negative emotional conditions like intense and chronic anxiety and depression (and likely a range of problems like eating disorders and even psychosis), plus better concentration and less distractedness (which itself has been found to increase negative moods). Another bonus: less mind-wandering and better focus leads to better learning, as attested by scores on exams.

In sum, instructions for cultivating essence love build on the handshake practice, leveraging this self-acceptance to access the basic spark of okayness we bring with us into our lives, the natural home of our emotional world. Essence love gives us a way to avoid being trapped in our thoughts of self-judgment by recognizing, restoring, and nurturing our natural well-being. Unlike self-help methods that stay at the level of verbal self-appreciation, building our essence love gives us a way to nurture the quality of basic well-being beneath the ups and downs of our thoughts and emotions. And that puts us in touch with our inner sense of okayness.

As we'll see in the next chapter, essence love strengthens compassion for ourselves, a preliminary to compassion for everyone else.

SIX

— ◆ —

LOVE AND COMPASSION

TSOKNYI RINPOCHE: THE EXPLANATION

I was asked recently, "How did you learn about love?"

The kind of love I learned about from all my teachers—from my grandfather to all the great masters I met—was very different from "normal" love. The flavor of love and compassion was there, but with a lot of openness, inclusiveness, and without judgment. They never said, "Oh, I love you; you're so great; you're wonderful." But they gave the greatest gift—they were including, open, and caring. I never felt like I was separated from my teachers. Somehow the feeling of my teachers' caring followed me like a shadow, wherever I went.

Even with my father, *I love you* was not something he would say. But also I didn't need to hear it. Openness, without any kind of sticky wanting or hidden agenda, is also love. It's more like a general sense of care. Nonjudging is also love. Love can arise in many other dimensions. It's not just concentrated on one area. I felt they were very open and caring and were willing for me to come back and see them anytime. They were so accessible. I never thought I needed an appointment to see them, or that my question for them might not be so good. Now I realize how special this was. Their caring was almost like space, not conditional like attached love. Space is the real love for all phenomena. Without this allowing quality of space, no phenomena could appear.

I actually learned about the narrower, concentrated kind of love later in my life, when I came to the West. It's conditional. This is also love, but it's very intense. Parenting love and romantic love are full of strong feelings—sweet and sour.

Everyone likes to talk about love and compassion. In a sense, love and compassion are some of the easiest and most natural topics in meditation and the spiritual path. They transcend any differences in philosophy, doctrine, or tradition. They can be a meeting point for different faiths and also between the secular and religious worlds. One subtlety is that from the Buddhist point of view, all sentient beings innately possess love and compassion. We can even say our true nature *is* love and compassion. Although we have this nature as our birthright, we can also cultivate these qualities deliberately. This is like stimulating something to come out, to grow and expand.

Nurturing love and compassion then becomes a dance between acknowledging the innate capacity and encouraging the various ways of cultivation, including looking at our ego and the ways it can obstruct and contaminate our love and compassion. In my tradition we make a big deal about something we call *bodhicitta*, which can be described as *vast unbiased altruism*. This is the gold standard of motivation, the most exquisite kind of intention that we aspire to. Before unbiased altruism can blossom, however, we must nurture the seeds of our love and compassion.

The Underlying Nature

The innate love and compassion that is at the core of our nature is like a sun contained in a shuttered house. It is always shining and radiating its natural warmth, but the house that contains it is shuttered quite tightly. The shutters represent our obscurations, such as self-centeredness, ego fixation, extreme attachment, bias, and aversion. Although the shutters block a lot of the light and warmth of the sun, they don't block all of it. Slivers of light and warmth escape through the cracks. These slivers are like the feelings and thoughts of love and compassion that we do have; the tenderness we have for our family and friends, our pets, the romantic love we can feel, and so on. Part of the practice is to come to understand and trust our innate nature of love and compassion, and another part of the practice is to work with removing the shutters of obscurations so that nature of love can shine and radiate freely to all beings.

Before I dive deeper into exploring the nature of love and compassion, let's look back at essence love. In the previous chapter we discussed essence love as a basic okayness, a natural well-being we are born with but which often gets covered up by layers of stress, self-judgment, and various emotional blockages. We hinted that essence love is the ground or seed of healthy *expression love*. The healthy way of expressing compassion or training in it is based on essence love.

Essence love helps minimize or reduce possible side effects of compassion, like getting depressed by others' suffering, or developing hatred toward perpetrators. We can get depressed because seeing suffering can trigger feelings of hollowness inside us. With essence love, we can channel our empathy and compassion into action and love, without the hollowness or the destructive energy of hatred. Without essence love, we can also become possessive and obsessed, or repeatedly get caught up in unhealthy, codependent relationships. Basically, our innate love and compassion can manifest in very obscured and limited ways. We can become biased and even deeply confused. Once we have healthy and grounded essence love, then love and compassion radiate naturally, with less baggage and fewer stories, less triggering of our wounds.

A key goal here is to be able to have love and compassion not only for those close to our hearts but also for our enemies. To achieve that we first need a foundation in essence love. Otherwise true compassion is on shaky ground. For example, a habitual pattern might boost our love and compassion, like being partial to a particular kind of dog, but this would be biased. Without the underlying warmth of essence love, our feelings and triggers turn into biased love and biased compassion. This is why essence love is so crucial as the ground for healthy love and compassion.

In brief, healthy love is with essence love, while unhealthy love lacks that foundation. This is delicate. I'm not trying to pass judgment on people for having "unhealthy" love and compassion. I want to point out ways that we all struggle to express our potential. Because attachment, jealousy, and possessiveness are often swirling around love and compassion, we all have to deal with a mixed cocktail of emotions.

Sometimes you are in the midst of experiencing love but don't know if it's healthy or not. You can use mindfulness to tell, being aware of the situation and of your feelings of love. For example, you meet someone you are interested in romantically. You feel excitement, possibility, fantasy, a tinge of jealousy about their other options—a swirling mixture of feelings. Try to bring awareness back from the person to your feeling world and be aware of these feelings in themselves. Then reconnect with essence love and ground yourself in your own basic okayness. Then again look at the feeling of love.

Is there bias or no bias? Is there anger or not? If you are connected with essence love, there will be much less bias and anger. Of course, a little bit of a normal range of attachment or jealousy is present with our love. But there can also be too much. If you feel there is too much, reconnect with essence love, and then express from there. With essence love, we will not be imbalanced;

our attachment and jealousy won't be out of control. This is a big difference!

With essence love you feel secure and an absence of hollowness. There's also an intelligence that saves us from extremes. For example, let's say I feel love toward my fiancée. But now another guy is looking at her. I can feel very jealous and angry. But if I have essence love, then there is some security. I can say to myself, *Okay, I feel these things. But it's okay. He has eyes; he can look. It's no big deal.* It's essence love talking to your own insecurity.

The root of Buddhism is wanting to have happiness and well-being, for ourselves and for others. We want everyone to feel that, to have the same opportunity. So we train in various reasons that all human beings are basically the same: we are all equal in wanting happiness and in wanting not to suffer. Traditionally we call this line of thinking a *lojong*, which means "mind-training." His Holiness the Dalai Lama is a great proponent of this, as is my old friend Sharon Salzberg, a great teacher of loving-kindness practice.

Although there are many ways to categorize happiness, and even though happiness looks different for different people, there is still some common happiness we can call "ethical": happiness and well-being that doesn't harm others. Ethical happiness is close to the basic well-being of essence love. Unfortunately, some people have more opportunity for this and some have less opportunity; some experience more suffering, and some experience more happiness. Loving kindness is to feel love for those who have less opportunity, even though they have the same right to be happy, to thrive. Love is wishing them to have the fruit of happiness.

Levels of Expression Love

Love is a complex topic, and even the word has many connotations. We have a variety of terms in our tradition, like the word *metta* (Sanskrit, *Maitrī*), which is often translated as *loving kindness*, *benevolence*, or *goodwill*. These definitions help distinguish it from more ordinary associations of possessive love. We also have other words that are similar to the English words *care* and *affection*.

I like to think about love as a multilevel phenomenon. Essence love is the foundation, the soil. From that ground, various kinds of expression love sprout and bloom in our relationships and spiritual practice. For example, we can have parental love, brotherly and sisterly love, romantic love, friendship love, devotional love, compassionate love, and so forth. All of these have some texture of essence love, the moisture of essence love. Essence love is like the eyes of love, while expression love is like the body, arms, and legs. Or we could say essence love is like the capacity or underlying warmth, while expression love is the enactment, the color and shape of the flames, what you actually see.

The healthy forms of expression love make life meaningful and joyful, and they are also the support that helps us survive when life is tough. These forms of love are often bound up with attachment, but that's normal. We can perhaps imagine a love beyond attachment, a deep and refined quality of unbiased love and compassion. This means we aren't limited to feeling love and compassion to particular people or groups, such as family, friends, or "my people," or victims. We can feel it for *everyone*, including enemies, strangers, and even perpetrators. This is a tough aspiration but something we can train in. The culmination of such unbiased love and compassion is *bodhicitta*, which is *vast universal altruism*.

Love can arise based either on feeling or on reasoning, and both are important and can be cultivated. We need both together in order to move toward unbiased love and compassion. Without feeling, pure reason can become dry, lacking warmth and tenderness. Just repeating loving phrases and aspirations can become mechanical if we don't feel connected to what we're saying. Pure feeling, however, without thinking and reasoning, can be limited and reactive, because our feelings often come out of our habitual patterns. Reasoning can elevate the love and compassion beyond its feeling-based roots into something vaster. For example, we feel a tinge of affection for our pet, which is beautiful but limited in itself to just this one being. With training, we can use the feeling of affection as a basis for expanding our love to include more and more beings. *Why wouldn't all beings deserve the same tenderness I feel for my pet? They do deserve it!* We can boost our affection and let our heart be filled with more and more compassion.

The Obstacles to Love and Compassion

There are many emotional obstacles to love and compassion, but we can condense them to three: attachment, indifference, and aversion. Attachment is a tricky one. Love is often bound up with attachment. This word can be confusing because modern psychology uses it to mean a positive quality; *secure attachment* is important during childhood and beyond. Buddhists agree that feeling safe and secure in our primary relationships is very important for a child; for anyone, in fact. However, we usually use the term *attachment* in a different sense. We use it to point to an unhealthy kind of extreme grasping, a limiting and sticky pattern: *I love you because you're mine. I love you because you make me happy.*

There is often confusion about this issue because it can then be assumed that good Buddhists should be "detached," but this can easily be misunderstood as some sort of numb indifference, a spaced-out person who just doesn't care about other people. But in my opinion this is a big mistake. Buddhist practice that is thorough and balanced should lead us to care a lot. Not just for our families and friends, but for everyone. We can develop a deep courage to look at suffering and open our hearts to anyone. So please understand the tradition and don't think that being indifferent and not caring is some sort of sign of spiritual aptitude or accomplishment. It's not. It just means you're numb and aloof and haven't shaken hands with those beautiful monsters—and you may be using your misunderstanding as an excuse. Please don't do that.

Having said that, we shouldn't feel too bad that our love and compassion is mixed with attachment; this is completely normal. It is something to be aware of though. We might shower our pets with sweetness and feel intense affection for them, but if someone accidently steps on their toes, we might feel like smacking or yelling at them. We generally love the people who love us, who are kind to us, who help us, who make us feel good. But attachment can make our love and compassion slip into bias, into preferences and prejudices. *I love this kind of people, but not that kind. I feel compassion for her, but not for him.* These feelings are normal but limiting. Although it's wonderful that we feel love and compassion for some beings, our world is still split between those we feel for and those we don't, the loved and unloved.

Indifference is another major obstacle that can show up as feeling neutral to strangers or even distant acquaintances. We might feel it doesn't really matter what happens to them. We may not wish them any harm, but we don't particularly care either, because we don't know them. We might be thinking, *It's hard enough to manage the complex relationships I have, let alone worrying about all the strangers too!* But these beings are just as worthy of our love and compassion as those we do know and care about. All these beings also suffer unnecessarily.

One of the biggest obstacles to feeling a vast sense of love or compassion is simple aversion. There are many flavors of aversion; more mild ones like dislike and irritation, and more intense ones like anger, hatred, and furious rage. There can be many reasons, of course, to feel these emotions, and sometimes they seem quite justified (*He harmed me!*) and sometimes they seem more random (*I just don't like people who talk loudly. Or people who wear baggy clothes.*). If we think about the behaviors we dislike, that irritate us, that have harmed us, we usually make an important assumption, whether consciously or not. *They did that on purpose. They knew what they were doing. They wanted to harm me, or irritate me. They should know better.*

But if we look into this assumption, it starts to fall apart. If deep down we want others to be happy, doesn't it make sense they have the same wish too, deep down? *Okay*, we might say, *then why did they do that stupid, hurtful thing? What other explanation could there be for such annoying behavior?* Well, why do *we* do things *we* regret, actions that harm others? It could be an unintentional mistake, just carelessness, but often it's because we are overtaken by an afflictive emotion and we temporarily lose control of our body, speech, or mind. It's not exactly us who did that. Of course, it's not anyone else either. It happens *while overtaken by an afflictive emotion*. Why would it be any different for anyone else?

One powerful antidote to irritation, anger, and hatred is to consider that people who harm us or behave in ways we dislike are overcome by afflictive emotions. So actually, the fault doesn't exactly lie with them, as much as with the afflictive emotions. But we lump the whole thing together. In addition, our own bias and resistance can get mixed into the situation and can play an important role in how we react and feel. If we're already holding some resistance or some grievance toward someone, then it can take only a small thing for us to feel hurt and react. The person, their emotions, their actions and words, all seem to be one lump, and that lump is making us feel like an angry lump of hurt!

Actually, however, the person, their emotions, their actions, and their nature are all different dimensions. Just like we get overwhelmed by our afflictive emotions and act in ways we regret, that can harm others, so do they. Being overtaken by emotions, they are worthy of compassion. We generally understand this idea when it comes to children. When a child is having a meltdown, we usually can separate the child from the emotion and actions. But when an adult melts down, we forget to make this separation, thinking they should take more responsibility for their emotions.

If we can get to a point where we feel genuine compassion for everyone involved in a negative situation—the victim, the perpetrators, the bystanders—this is very powerful. It doesn't mean we lose our discernment and don't recognize right and wrong. We still know virtue and nonvirtue. It doesn't mean we become overly passive and don't protect those who need protection. If it's right to intervene, we should intervene and help protect. If we need to protect ourselves from mistreatment or abuse, we should do that too. But we can also feel compassion for everyone involved, and this is a powerful gift: not putting our own negative emotions like hatred or revenge into the situation. Cultivating compassion for those we dislike or find annoying, and even for those who have harmed us, gives us a very powerful opportunity for transformation.

The Distinction between Love and Compassion

Love and compassion are very similar, and we need both. Love is easier than compassion, because love focuses on goodness, while compassion has the courage to protect from suffering. Love wishes others well, wants others to flourish—to have well-being, joy, health, success, virtue, and all that is desirable and good.

Compassion, on the other hand, focuses on the widespread suffering in this world and wishes to relieve it, both for yourself and for others. Compassion focuses on safety. Compassion sees all kinds of suffering: physical, mental, emotional, social, and spiritual. Compassion is willing to look at old age, sickness, and death. Compassion sees fear, anxiety, depression, loneliness, and so on. Compassion is one of the most beautiful and profound capacities we have. In one sense compassion is very simple; we encounter suffering directly or indirectly and feel an urge to relieve it.

In cultivating compassion, however, things can get more complex. When we look at the suffering in the world it can feel almost unbearable; we might feel overwhelmed, that it's just too much to bear. Looking at suffering can also trigger wounds and beautiful monsters in our own mind, making us feel heaviness and even depression. When we are repeatedly exposed to pain and suffering, it can keep pulling us down. That's one reason many nurses, doctors, therapists, social workers, and other people in helping professions can get burned-out. So compassion needs a little understanding mixed in, to stay balanced.

For example, we need realistic expectations for ourselves. We do whatever we can, despite feeling like we need to do everything. To expect ourselves—or anyone—to help beyond their ability is not wise. Simply put, we cannot give more than we have. Still, if we don't use the ability we do have, that is not compassion. We need a sense of balance between what we wish we could do and what's actually possible for us.

The wisdom of understanding *impermanence*—that nothing is solid and unchanging—can be helpful in avoiding being overwhelmed and pulled down by compassion. However bad things are, they are not permanent. Every condition is bound to change into something else. The wisdom of seeing *interdependence* can also be very helpful. Everything is a result of causes and conditions; everything depends on many other things. Whatever happens, at some basic level, is just a temporary occurrence arising due to the coming together of the necessary causes and conditions. This can help us get out of the blame game, and out of victim mentality.

Willingness to Suffer

Sometimes I hesitate to talk about genuine compassion. It's so precious, but it also has many impostors. Sometimes I tell of "California compassion"—I like to tease people who live in California because it's so beautiful there. I may or may not have made this story up. One night a nice spiritual man living in California was getting ready for bed. He lit some incense and did a few minutes of "compassion meditation" before climbing under his soft organic sheets. He wanted to feel fresh and look good the next morning at work, so he was looking forward to a good, restful sleep. But then the phone rang. A friend was feeling really sick and asked if the man could take her to the hospital. He took a deep breath. Part of him wanted to be the kind of person who did that, but he also really wanted to sleep well and feel fresh in the morning. The desire for good rest won, and he apologized in a soothing voice and said he couldn't do it, but he really hoped she found someone to take her, *really hoped she felt better*.

When the phone call ended, he crawled back under his sheets

and tried to go to sleep. But feelings of guilt kept coming up, and he tossed and turned for a while. *Maybe I should have helped her. . . . I would want my friends to help me if I was sick. . . . I guess I could go there now and see if she is okay. . . .* But he still didn't want to get dressed, drive out into the night, and deal with the bright lights of the hospital. After a while, the guilty and conflicted feelings got so strong that he got up, put on his soft organic robe, and went back to his cozy meditation cushion. He breathed deeply in and out, *sending his friend compassion and healing energy*. After a while he felt better and was able to fall asleep.

While the breathing practice and his prayers could *seem* compassionate, his intention was to pacify his own guilty feelings and be able to sleep. His motivation was about his own well-being. That is the practice of "California compassion."

We have a right to have boundaries and to take care of ourselves. But we shouldn't call what he did *an act of compassion*. That isn't fair to genuine acts of compassion. We should call what he did *self-care*—he took care of himself. The difference in my mind is *being willing to suffer*. Deeper compassion involves a willingness to be uncomfortable, a willingness to suffer, in order to benefit others. This takes some guts; courage is a big deal in the topic of love and compassion. It's what breaks us out of limiting beliefs, emotional patterns, and fear. In any particular situation, we may suffer or we may not suffer, but compassion is willing to suffer. The benefit of others becomes more important than avoiding discomfort for ourselves. This is something most parents, especially of young children, express every day. But we can also train in this attitude and strengthen the seeds within us.

The Practice

In handshake practice we learned to heal the connection between our mind and feeling world. One result of that connection is good communication. We can harness it for healing and nurturing our essence love. But we can also use it to develop our love and compassion. When there is a good connection, we can generate an expansive, compassionate thought and allow it to fill our feeling world, radiating outward. We can also have a feeling and then upgrade or expand it with our thinking.

TRY IT FOR A LITTLE WHILE: sit comfortably and settle into your body and feeling world. Try to connect with the basic well-being of essence love. Now think: *How wonderful it would be if all beings could have happiness, could be safe, could thrive, could get what they wish for!* Try to allow this thought to permeate your feeling world and then send it outward in every direction as an aspiration.

Mind-Training

In my tradition we greatly cherish the practice of *lojong*, which means "mind-training." This is where we roll up our sleeves and actually challenge our ego, using logic and reasoning, courage, and persistence. After all, it's our ego, with its self-centeredness and tunnel vision, that is the main reason our love and compassion get covered up, and why they slip into biases and prejudices when they get expressed. We are just referring to the ordinary "ego," the self-referencing sense of "me first" that tends toward flipping back and forth between self-aggrandizement and self-deprecation. The ego usually cherishes *my* needs, and those people and things that I consider "mine," over those that are considered "others." We often sum up this self-cherishing as: *me, my, and mine*. I like to think of this as an inner song we sing to ourselves most of the day: "Me, me, it's all about me. . . ."

There are many types of mind-training, but three are particularly beneficial for countering our self-cherishing. These are *equalizing self and other*, *exchanging self and other*, and *cherishing others more than oneself*. The first one, *equalizing self and other*, involves contemplating the basic equality of myself and other beings. Remember, we are all the same in wanting happiness and not to suffer. It doesn't matter if we're old or young, rich or poor, educated or not. All our differences in gender, race, background, sexual preferences, religion, nationality, and ethnicity are equalized at this basic human level. Of course these differences can be very significant at other levels, but despite all these varieties of experience, fundamentally we all have the same basic platform of existence—we all must face birth, old age, sickness, and death. These are the basic ground rules of life—we are all brothers and sisters in birth, old age, sickness, and death.

Equalizing Self and Other

Begin by taking a comfortable posture and relaxing with awareness. Contemplate that you yourself deep down want to be happy and want not to suffer. Now contemplate that others deep down want to be happy and want not to suffer. Consider that in this regard, yourself and others are exactly the same. Allow all the surface-level differences to dissolve in the deep recognition of the basic equality of yourself and all beings. Consider that all beings have the basic right to be happy. Allow a sense of deep care and compassion to well up for all beings, and extend it outward, wishing them well.

Exchanging Self and Other

The second mind-training is *exchanging self and other*. It's like imagining walking a mile in someone else's shoes. You put yourself in their place, their mind, their life. You imagine their feelings, thoughts, and struggles. The more you understand them, the more you "wear their shoes." If they do something bad to you, you can understand their issues, where they are coming from, why they are angry. If you practice this well, you almost become like them. Seeing their situation, you look at the interdependence and you understand their condition and motivations more and more. The more you understand the situation of others, the more sympathy and empathy you will feel. This mind-training can also help us cut through and diminish emotions like pride and envy.

When we don't feel compassion toward a situation, it's often because we don't understand that situation very well. One drawback of exchanging self and other is we won't know whom to blame. Most lives are full of suffering; that is why someone behaves badly. We will not agree with their actions, but we don't need to hate them. We can feel compassion, while definitely not agreeing with their actions. Their actions come from ignorance, but this ignorance is not coming from their choice—it's beyond their control. If we internalize all of this, then real solid hatred will not arise. Some brief anger can arise but not lasting hatred. We will see all harm coming from ignorance.

Exchanging Self and Other

✦ · · ✦ · · ✦

Begin by relaxing with awareness. Bring to mind someone in a difficult situation. Imagine putting yourself in their position. Imagine how you would feel. Imagine the mental, emotional, and physical struggles you might have. Allow a deep care and compassion to wash over your being. Extend those feelings first to that person and then to all beings. Repeat with many different people in many different situations. This is particularly helpful when someone is challenging for you.

✦

Cherishing Others More Than Oneself

The third mind-training is called *cherishing others more than oneself*. This involves contemplating how many "others" there are in the world, and how many "me." Not so surprisingly, we reflect that there is one "me," billions of other people, and countless other beings. Then we ask, *Which is more important, the happiness of one being, or the happiness of countless beings?* We sit with this contemplation until a deep concern for others wells up from within. This helps reduce various kinds of selfishness and self-centeredness.

Begin by relaxing into awareness. Reflect on how many beings there are in the world, human and animal, and how many of you there are. Ask yourself the question, *Which is more important, the happiness of one being or the happiness of countless beings?* Think of all the care and concern you have for yourself. Imagine that spiraling outward instead of inward, directed toward the service of all beings.

Gratitude

Let yourself realize how your body is the products of others. You were literally made by others. Every meal, every glass of water, every opportunity you've had that has sustained you, comes from the kindness of others. Consider that you could not exist or survive without them.

REFLECT: How wonderful it would be if I could repay the kindness of others! How wonderful it would be if my body, my mind, my energy, and all my efforts were beneficial to others! May everything I do be a cause for the happiness and freedom of others!

Handshake and Expression Love

A frequent question is "If we still have a lot of beautiful monsters to handshake, can we still express compassion—try to help others?"

Yes! It's definitely okay to do both at the same time. As long as we are aware of our beautiful monsters and keep trying to connect with essence love, we can keep helping others. We might need a little extra caution, a little extra mindfulness to avoid the bad side effects—such as our compassion triggering feelings of hollowness, hatred, or revenge. The road may be good or bad, but we still drive. If the road is rough and bumpy, we just need extra awareness, extra care.

This practice has two basic parts—reconnecting with essence love repeatedly, whenever we need, as a foundation, and the actual trainings in love and compassion. Ideally, we will alternate these meditations and reflections so that essence love is the foundation of the other meditations. Whenever you cannot connect with essence love, engage whatever is coming up with the handshake practice. These contemplations and meditations are meant to be repeated many times.

✦ · · ✦ · · ✦

As before, take a comfortable posture, sitting or lying down, with your back straight, while being as relaxed as possible. Begin by dropping awareness into the body. Allow the embodied awareness to extend to the feeling world for a little while. Try to connect with the basic okayness underlying the feeling world. Try to notice a subtle warmth or well-being underneath anything that is happening on the surface of the feeling world. If you can connect with essence love, allow it to suffuse your whole being. Nurture your connection to essence love. If you cannot connect, don't worry, handshake whatever is happening. Come back to this again and again.

Then, reflection on beings close to your heart

Take a comfortable posture as before and relax into awareness. Bring to mind some person or animal that you have love, tenderness, or affection toward. Allow the feelings to well up and fill your feeling world. Now allow the image of that being to dissolve and allow the loving feelings to remain. Then try to extend those feelings to other beings, first a sphere of beings close to you, then a vaster and vaster sphere of more and more beings. Imagine how wonderful it would be to feel strong love, compassion, and affection for all beings, as you do for this particular being.

Reflection on neutral beings

Take a comfortable posture as before and begin by relaxing. Bring to mind a stranger or neutral being, some person or animal you don't have any particularly positive or negative feelings toward. Then try to generate a deep sense of care and concern for them: "May you be happy. May you be peaceful. May you be safe. May you thrive. May all your wishes be fulfilled." Notice how it feels to generate strong good wishes for a stranger or neutral being. Then bring to mind all the infinite strangers, the neutral beings in the world, and imagine how wonderful it would be to have deep concern, care, and compassion for all of them.

Reflection on difficult beings

Take a comfortable posture and relax with awareness. Bring to mind a being who is difficult for you, someone you dislike, an enemy, or someone who makes you angry. Try to contemplate their struggles, their situation, their suffering. They probably want to be a good person and make others feel good but are overwhelmed by their own afflictive emotions. Try to feel concern and compassion for them. Allow the compassion and care to well up and fill your feeling world. Imagine how wonderful it would be to have this care and compassion for all the difficult beings in the world.

◆

DANIEL GOLEMAN: THE SCIENCE

My wife, Tara, and I had the good fortune to spend a few weeks with Tsoknyi Rinpoche and one of his main teachers, Adeu Rinpoche. We were on the island of Putuoshan, a ferry's ride from the Chinese mainland, and not far from Shanghai.

Putuoshan, Tibetans say, is where Noble Tara, the goddess of compassion, resides; the Potala Palace in Lhasa, I've been told, takes its name from Putuoshan. For the Chinese that island houses the abode of Kuan Yin, their version of a compassionate goddess. Putuoshan has been a pilgrimage place for centuries.

As we were leaving our hotel to return home, we were approached by two Tibetan monks, one hobbling on a crude crutch. One of his legs had a horrible festering sore, and he needed money to pay a surgeon to amputate lest he die from infection. The monk said he needed, as I recall, around fifteen hundred yuan (the Chinese currency) to have enough for the surgery.

Without a second thought I took twelve hundred yuan out of my wallet—most of the cash I had with me—and gave it to him.

The look on Adeu Rinpoche's face told me he heartily approved of this act of charity.

The memory brings to mind a moment with Anagarika Munindra, a teacher in the Thai forest tradition who lived in Bodh Gaya, India, where the Buddha was enlightened. Munindra-ji was from the Bengali Barua caste, a group who say they have been Buddhist since the time of Buddha. When Munindra-ji saw my then-three-year-old son give money to beggars there, he said "Sadhu, sadhu, sadhu," indicating he was witnessing a praiseworthy act.

As he explained, giving charity like that benefits not just the receiver but also the giver, who displays generosity in doing so. And generosity is one of the *paramitas*, the much-lauded noble qualities of character in the Buddhist tradition.

Love or its many distortions and convolutions are central to much of contemporary psychology, particularly psychotherapy. The development of children, for instance, is looked at through the lens of "attachment theory," which analyzes patterns of security, anxious connection, or emotional avoidance that take shape in childhood in response to caretakers' ability—or lack of it. Loving well in this sense means to connect with the child to provide for their physical and emotional needs. Eventually, those emotional patterns are tracked into adulthood, where they emerge again in a person's love relationships.

But psychological science has little to say about the kinds of love and compassion that Rinpoche's practices help us develop. It's only in recent years, with the advent of positive psychology, that this branch of science has begun to explore compassion. At a 2003 Mind & Life meeting with scientists, the Dalai Lama challenged Richard Davidson to use his brain research tools to study compassion. But it wasn't until 2008 that Davidson was able to publish a scientific paper with the word *compassion* in its title.

The Dalai Lama had been urging psychologists to pursue this focus on a love without attachment for many years. Back in the 1980s at a conference with psychotherapists, the Dalai Lama was surprised to hear that a common problem in the West was people who were self-critical, even to the point of self-loathing. In his language and in the classic languages of his tradition—Sanskrit and Pali—the word *compassion* included oneself, but in English it included only other people. He said the English language needed a new word: *self-compassion*. This was years before an American psychologist, Kristin Neff, began her research on self-compassion.

As I've described in my book *Focus: The Hidden Driver of Excellence*, a scientific understanding of what's behind our compassionate acts starts with a key distinction between empathy and compassion. Research tells us the three varieties of empathy are each based in their own brain circuits.

The first of the most widely known sorts of empathy is *cognitive*, where I know how you see the world. I understand your perspective, can see things from your point of view, even know the language you use—technically, your "mental models." This lets me use words you will understand best; cognitive empathy makes communications go more smoothly.

The second kind of empathy is *emotional*: I know what you feel because I feel it too. This empathy activates brain circuits that are the focus of affective neuroscience, the study of how the brain takes in and responds to another person's emotions. While emotional empathy can create intense rapport, it can also lead to "empathy distress," feeling upset at the pain and suffering of others.

Empathy distress has become a widely recognized problem in fields like health care, where nurses, for example, encounter patients who are in pain, angry, or at their wit's end—and the nurse feels the patients' distress too. If that nurse feels this way day after day, week after week, it can lead to emotional exhaustion and burnout—and quitting the field. This loss of medical personnel to empathy distress has become a major dilemma in the health care world.

One way people handle their distress at seeing another person's suffering is by turning away, whether actually ignoring them or creating an inner psychological distance. The former strategy, turning a blind eye, is one of the most painful experiences reported by homeless people, who say they are literally not seen on the street. The second approach, emotional distancing, plagues professions like medicine, where staff handle the distress of patients via a psychological distance that fosters jokes, and indifference, but blocks caring.

Then there's the research on how meditation changes our ability to empathize. Studies of long-term meditators at the University of Wisconsin brain-imaging lab showed that when they saw pictures of people in dire distress—like a fire victim whose skin was burned off—their amygdala and related circuits flared up more than did those of people who were not meditators. This suggests that their own circuits for distress had become sensitized so that their emotional empathy was greater.

Our amygdala acts as a "salience" detector, making us pay attention to what's urgent, right now—like someone else in great distress. Along with the amygdala, another brain area—the insula—sends out messages to the body's organs, readying to respond to an emergency.

So instead of turning away to lessen their own upset, the meditators actually became more likely to help. What's going on here was made apparent by a series of studies at the Max Planck Institute in Germany, where a highly seasoned meditator, Matthieu Ricard, had his brain scanned while seeing photos of people, like that burn victim, in greatly distressing conditions.

When Ricard was asked to empathize with those suffering people, his own circuitry for pain lit up. But when he was then told to view them with compassion—having loving feelings toward their suffering—his brain activated circuits for positive emotions and feeling close to others.

This ability to stay present to another person's suffering seems to be a lasting benefit of practice. Seven years after volunteers took part in a three-month retreat, those who immediately afterward looked at pictures of suffering people, rather than turning away were still more able to witness such suffering.

Researchers at the institute, following this clue, then recruited volunteers to cultivating compassion in response to other people's suffering, in one group, and another group to simply empathize with them. The trained groups had similar brain patterns—emotional empathy increased their distressing feelings when confronted with suffering, while compassion lessened it.

The power of compassion lies in the third variety of empathy, which technically is called *empathic concern*. This sort of empathy activates a very different neural circuitry than the others: the brain's caretaking circuitry that we share with other mammals—it's a parent's love for a child. This is the circuitry that activates when we feel love for anyone—a partner, our family, our friends.

Think of a parent handling a small child who is having a tantrum. Instead of being angry in response to the child's anger, a loving parent can stay present to their distress while firmly setting boundaries in a kind way. That combination of presence plus caring seems to be trainable, if someone pursues a practice that cultivates compassion. These circuits grow stronger, even with short bouts of compassion training.

This high responsivity to the suffering of others, along with caring, also can be found in an unusual group: people who donate a kidney to save the life of a stranger. These paragons of compassion, brain scans reveal, tend to have an enlarged area in their amygdala that seems to make them more sensitive than others to someone else's suffering. This empathy seems to lead to their act of outstanding altruism.

Cultivating compassion has positive payoffs beyond enhancing empathy. For instance, the Davidson lab at the University of Wisconsin divided participants randomly into two groups, one that reflected on the cause of their emotional problems, and another that practiced a compassion exercise. Afterward the compassion group was twice as generous on a test of generosity.

As little as two and a half hours of compassion practice on-line shows similar benefits. Compared with a group of volunteers who spent the same amount of time doing stretching routines, those who cultivated compassion were far more likely to donate to a charity afterward.

These benefits seem specific to compassion cultivation, in whatever form it takes, rather than to other kinds of meditation. If someone does a meditation that sharpens their meta-awareness of their thoughts and feelings, for instance, the circuitry for that kind of attention grows stronger but not their altruism. The bottom line: if you want to become kinder and more caring, practice compassion.

There's an unexpected bonus from feeling compassion: our brain's circuitry for happiness activates, making the one who feels compassion feel good about it. The Dalai Lama often says, "The first person to benefit from compassion is the one who feels it."

Even very short bouts of compassion seem to boost a person's sense of connection to other people, as well as having their brain display the beginning of neural changes in those who have practiced compassion methods for years. We seem to have a "biological preparedness" for warmheartedness, akin to a child's knack for learning language. The more hours over a lifetime someone does a compassion cultivation practice, the more generous and caring they seem to become.

In many Asian countries people revere Kuan Yin, a goddess of compassion; in Tibet the equivalent would be Noble Tara. Her name translates as "the one who listens and hears the cry of the world in order to come help."

——— ✦ ———

SEVEN

CALM AND CLEAR

TSOKNYI RINPOCHE: THE EXPLANATION

Many years ago, Danny invited me to high tea at a fancy hotel in San Francisco. I had just come from India. When I entered the hotel no one treated me like a stranger. Where I come from they examine you head to toe, even the waiters. It's quite uncomfortable for a few minutes. Everyone is looking at you. In my country staring directly at people is no problem. Then when you sit down, one waiter comes, takes your order, and then they are gone. Gone means gone. They take your order and then they go their way. No one is checking on you. If you need something else, you have to look for them, you have to shout.

In San Francisco they didn't ask many questions. They were very quiet and polite, not obvious, no staring. I was about to sit down, and suddenly one guy behind me pulled out the chair for me. I was looking around because it was all new to me. I didn't see any obvious waiter—no one was hanging around. But as soon as I looked around someone was right there: "Sir, do you need anything?" They were not in our faces but somehow they were watching from afar, mindfully aware of us. This was the second surprise.

I was already curious how they would bring the food. In India food often comes in a bit of a messy way, waiters always bumping into each other. I thought, *How are they going to serve the food?* Three waiters came, carrying plates elegantly. There was no bumping, and they placed the dishes perfectly. They were always aware of one another. They were so mindful I thought, *Wow. I've learned about mindfulness practice, but this is the place where it happens.*

The waiters showed panoramic awareness and intent mindfulness, narrow and broad together. The "narrow" was when they put the soup in exactly the right place on the table; the "broad" was that they were also aware of who was behind them. If they had only the narrow, they might put the soup down correctly but lose track of what was happening behind them. If they had only the broad, they might be aware of the whole area, but not place things precisely. But they had both.

We can benefit from this kind of practice in general. It would solve so many problems. Sometimes we actually bump into things—but mostly we bump into situations and other people.

Everyday mindfulness could help with difficulties that come from unawareness.

At this point we have spent a lot of time discussing the body and the feeling world. We talked about dropping and relaxing into the body, about stress and energy, about handshaking feelings and emotions, and about connecting with our intrinsic essence love, our basic well-being. Now it's time to talk about the mind. The mind is of course the big focus in meditation. Traditionally it often comes first, but I like to start with the body and work our way through the feeling world to the mind.

I think this makes it less likely we will bypass or skip over our feeling world and emotions. My friend John Welwood was a therapist who taught about *spiritual bypass*, using methods like meditation to avoid painful emotional realities. Bypassing can lead to all kinds of spiritual, emotional, and social problems—and it doesn't work anyway. So the earlier chapters were designed to help us connect with our bodies and feeling worlds in an honest and grounded way. Now we have to deal with our minds as well.

To work with the mind it helps to first understand a little about our mental workings. In my tradition there are many ways the mind is described—in fact there are thousands of pages of categories and descriptions, some that are profound and precise, some of which I also refer to when I teach. But I don't think we need to know all of that to work with the mind. We just need a practical model so we can get started.

The Four Expressions of Mind

While there are many models of the mind, I find a simple model, based on traditional ideas, the most useful. Sometimes too many intellectual concepts just get in the way.

Basically, the mind expresses itself in four different ways: *knowing*, *thinking*, *awareness*, and *clarity*. *Knowing* is automatic. Once we learn something, we automatically know it: a red flower is both red and a flower. Most of the time, we don't need to re-learn and reanalyze the world. Such knowing happens constantly, subconsciously, by itself. Even if we are focused on another task, when an airplane flies overhead, we automatically know it's an airplane; the sound is associated with a label we already learned.

Thinking is straightforward, we all know what thinking is. We are all experts at this; millions of thoughts come and go through our minds every day. But there is an important distinction between deliberately thinking about something and when thoughts arise by themselves. Sometimes we actively engage in deliberate thought—*we think about something*. Other times thoughts just pop up in the mind. In my tradition, when thoughts just pop up, we consider them like a sense object, like a sound or a smell.

Awareness is where things get more subtle. Mindfulness comes out of awareness. Mindfulness involves a little effort of noticing. Sometimes I call it *double knowing*—we know that we're knowing something. We are knowing the flower, but we can also be mindful that we're knowing the flower. Mindfulness is almost the same as awareness, but awareness also has the potential to be either intimate or panoramic. We all have awareness, but it doesn't always manifest this potential. Through deliberate effort mindfulness becomes one with awareness. We will refer to these terms interchangeably in this chapter because they are so similar.

Clarity is the unique quality of our mind that distinguishes it from other phenomena. Clarity is like the basic substance of the mind; it is the raw material that makes up knowing, thinking, and awareness. Here clarity doesn't mean how we normally think of it—*She has a lot of clarity*, or *Their thinking is really clear*. It is rather something more fundamental, *the basic backdrop of the mind*—a wakeful quality. When we look into the raw material of the mind itself, it's not dull and dark. There is a luminous quality. We can experience drowsiness and darkness because of this clarity. Without clarity, we couldn't experience drowsiness, the dimming of clarity. According to my tradition, the uniqueness of clarity defines the mind. Other phenomena, apart from mind, don't have this basic, luminous clarity.

Mindful Awareness

The main tool of practice is *mindful awareness*. Awareness has two qualities—*aware of other* and *aware of itself*. *Aware of other* means it is aware of objects, both tangible things like sense objects and intangible things like thoughts and mental states. *Aware of itself* means it knows its own qualities. For me, the purpose of mindfulness practice is to become mindful of awareness—of itself.

Otherwise, we might still have the capacity of awareness but we may not be mindful of it. For example, we have reading glasses, but if we don't remember to wear our glasses then they don't help us. If we are not mindful of our awareness, we still have it but it's of no use. Without mindfulness, awareness doesn't become part of our path, because although it's there, we are not utilizing it. So mindfulness allows us to utilize our intrinsic awareness.

So if mindfulness is important, what is it exactly and how can we train in it? In the Buddhist world, mindfulness is taught in every tradition. There are many descriptions and many definitions. In my tradition, mindfulness is usually described as *remembering, noticing, or bringing attention to something again and again*. It's very simple in a way. A carpenter is mindful of the wood and the blade. A cook is mindful of temperature, flavor, texture, timing, and so on while preparing a meal. We naturally use mindfulness all the time when doing this and that. But what about when we're not performing a task?

In other words, what is mindfulness like on its own? And how can we train it? Traditionally we talk about the *four foundations of mindfulness*—mindfulness of *body*, *sensations*, *mind*, and *mental formations*, like thoughts and images. These are the domains where we can establish mindfulness. Mindfulness means training the mind in simple, undistracted attention. We can start with anything—the movement of our legs as we walk, say—and build it up to include everything we experience. To put it in plain language, with mindfulness we become more and more present, more and more aware of what is happening in us and around us. The new habit of mindfulness slowly replaces the old habit of being distracted or checked out, lost in thoughts about the past and future.

Thoughts and emotions can be a challenge, and mindfulness helps a lot with getting space around and inside them. If you know you're angry, you are mindful of anger. To use the example from my brother Mingyur Rinpoche, if you can see the river, you are not drowning in the river. To put it another way, if you're aware you're distracted, you are no longer distracted. Eventually we can become mindful of awareness, and then mindfulness and awareness become indivisible. Mindfulness is awareness, and awareness is mindful. Then our practice is almost on autopilot. From time to time, we might need mindfulness to switch on, and then awareness takes over. At that point, we don't need to hold on to mindfulness, because the job of mindfulness will be done by awareness.

When we reach awareness in this way, we become much more relaxed. Our minds become more panoramic and more inclusive. Ordinarily, mindfulness is narrower and focus oriented, mindful of some object (even a thought can be an object of such mindfulness). But we need to start from mindfulness. As we move toward awareness, it becomes less narrowly focused, less object-targeting. The culmination of this process is experiencing *unconfined lucid openness* more and more. Training starts from the narrow and then dissolves into the broad. There are still elements of the narrow, such as the precision, together with the broadness. Something I've noticed while teaching in the West is when people become broad they can think they have lost the mindfulness. Then they come out of the broad and become narrow again. So we need to know that *beyond being mindful* . . . is awareness.

The Shepherd, the Sheep, and the Rope

A lot of the meditators in my tradition came from nomadic back-grounds in Tibet, where many people are herders and shepherds, cowboys of the high plateau. So they really liked metaphors involving livestock. This practice of *mindful awareness* is described using an old-fashioned example of sheep tied to a pole with rope, watched over by a shepherd. Our minds are like the sheep. Mindfulness is like the rope. Awareness is like the shepherd. Like sheep, our minds sometimes stay calm and sometimes get restless and wander around. The rope is a direct way to tether them to a point. Mindfulness of breathing, sensations, and so forth is like a rope tethering our minds to a support and providing a boundary of how far it can move. The shepherd's perspective is more panoramic, keeping an eye on the whole situation but not tightly focused on the particular steps of any particular sheep. Awareness is panoramic, keeping track of the whole situation in a relaxed, open way.

After establishing a habit of mindful awareness, the next step is *settling and focusing*—sometimes called *calm-abiding*, or *resting in undistracted tranquility*. This step, known as *shamata* in Sanskrit (and *shiney* in Tibetan), is a widespread and beloved practice across all Buddhist traditions. There are two essential methods here: *settling with an object*, and *settling without an object*. The point of both of these is to become *calm*, *clear*, *undistracted*, and *pliable*. The practice uses mindfulness to keep bringing your attention back to the object (for example, your breath), until your mind settles more and more one-pointedly.

This takes time and patience, because we are not used to this kind of relaxed focusing.

With the body and feeling-based practices up until this chapter, we have been practicing in a very open, welcoming way toward whatever happens. With *shamata* we are learning to say yes and no to different aspects of our experience. We are establishing a *view*, a perspective we are maintaining. In a sense we're saying no to distraction and saying yes to settling and focusing. We're repeatedly picking our chosen object over any other possible object the mind could engage with.

Nowness

Settling without an object is more subtle. We don't even have an object as an anchor but rather just settle with a sense of nowness, allowing whatever is happening to happen, while remaining undistractedly aware in the present moment.

The *view* or *perspective* we're cultivating here is *clear, thought-free nowness*. It is *clear* because the basic clarity of the mind is being recognized and sustained. It is *thought-free* because the practice isn't a deliberate act of pondering and actively thinking about something. A key point is that *thought-free* here doesn't mean there will be no thoughts popping up at all. It means *the practice itself isn't an act of thinking*.

Thoughts are allowed to pop up naturally and subside naturally, like sounds or clouds in the sky or bubbles on the surface of water. But the view we're sustaining isn't a discursive thought.

It is just the naturally clear, thought-free awareness of nowness. Thoughts can and will pop up and dissolve as a part of nowness. We can sustain this view with or without an object of focus.

Remember that it's completely normal to constantly get distracted when we begin to work with the mind in this way. We don't need to get dramatic when we get distracted, just gently bring the mind back to the object. We don't need to judge ourselves; we don't need to finish any of these thoughts. As soon as we notice we're distracted we are already mindful again, so we can just bring the mind back. We don't need to believe the thoughts: *I'm just a bad meditator. Maybe other people can do this, but I just can't.* These thoughts are normal but not true. If judgments come up, and feelings of failure or wanting to give up, try to handshake them. It is fine to alternate handshake and settling practice. We may have to bring the mind back hundreds of thousands of times. We are creating a new habit—it takes diligence, patience, and repetition.

At first, we may be able to stay with the object for only one or two seconds. This is normal. Slowly our ability to be undistracted will get longer and longer. At some point we approach *one-pointedness*, which is also described as *unification*. This training has many beneficial effects, such as calmness and focus. Another outcome is *pliability*, which means that the mind is no longer under the power of whatever thoughts, sensations, and perceptions happen to occur. It has found its own independence and stability; it is no longer dominated by other factors. If we want to place our mind on something, we can. If we want it to shift to something else and stay there we also can. Our wild mind has become tamed.

Hindrances

The main hindrances to settling and focusing are *agitation* and *dullness*. Agitation is when the mind is very energized. It feels wild and feisty, and wanders all over the place. It is full of thoughts, shooting into the past and future, and we feel an urge to jump up from the cushion and do a thousand things. This is very common. Many of us live fast-paced, highly stimulated lifestyles. Our minds have become normalized to this, and when we sit down to watch our breath and relax, the mind doesn't easily calm down.

The opposite hindrance is dullness, when the mind has low energy. It feels drowsy and sluggish, as though a thick layer of mental fog has set in. We want to fall asleep or numb ourselves by watching TV. Dullness is also very common. After being highly stimulated and stressed, when we sit down and try to settle and focus, the mind has a residue of tiredness that manifests as dullness and drowsiness.

The stages of experience we go through in this training are described using the metaphor of a stream cascading down from the mountains until it merges with a lake. First there is a mountain waterfall, then a rushing stream, then a meandering, gentle river, and finally a placid lake. These stages reflect how our minds experience the flow of thought movement during our training. When we start to practice mindfulness of thoughts, it can seem like the busyness of the mind has gotten worse. There seems to be a constant and overwhelming onslaught of thoughts. This is called the *waterfall experience*. We might think, *My mind wasn't this busy and wild before I started meditating. It couldn't have been!* Actually, it has not gotten worse, we have just gotten more aware of what was already there. The waterfall experience is a good sign; it means we are actually starting to work with the mind.

After some time, the intensity of thoughts starts to calm down a little. It's still quite busy but not as overwhelming. We can start to experience some space sometimes. This is called the *rushing stream experience*. If we keep working with our mind, it will continue to calm down, slow down, and more and more space will be present among our thoughts. This is called the *meandering river experience*. Our mind has become quite calm at this point. If we keep training, eventually the thoughts will really slow down a lot, and we will have sustained experiences of stillness: clear, thought-free nowness. This is called the *placid lake experience*, and it is seen as the beginning of one-pointedness or unification. While not everyone has this experience, anyone who diligently and persistently trains their minds can experience this level of settling.

Some Practical Tips

Essentially, we are establishing a habit of being *calm and clear*. Another way to put this is that we are learning how to be *relaxed and alert* at the same time. Normally, when we start to relax, we slip into dullness—like sinking into a couch with the TV controller, or sitting on a beach and dozing off. When we are alert, we often feel slightly tight, agitated, or anxious. It is rare we are relaxed and alert at the same time. We may not even know this is possible. Forming this new habit takes patience. A key point of training to keep in mind: *short moments, many times*. When we find this quality of being calm and clear, relaxed and alert, it usually doesn't last very long. *We need quality, not just quantity.* Many people imagine that a "good meditator" should sit in perfect peace for long periods of time. But this isn't what the training actually looks like. When we try to meditate for long periods of time, we usually stray into distraction and dullness quite quickly. It is far more effective to practice for short periods of higher quality, fresh mindful awareness. For example, within a twenty- or thirty-minute session, it is usually more effective to practice multiple three- to five-minute sessions, with a short break of a minute or so between them. Our ability to remain fresh will slowly and organically increase over time. This happens through repetition and habituation, not willpower.

Another important point is to remain balanced, *not too tight and not too loose*. If we're too tight, we'll lose our calmness and relaxation. If we're too loose, we'll stray into distraction. It's like tuning a guitar. For the best sound it should be tuned just right— not too tight and not too loose. This is something we will slowly feel for ourselves over time. We will need to adjust our practice many, many times to find this natural balance.

When sustaining mindful awareness, agitation and dullness will definitely happen from time to time. These are not personal failings; they happen to pretty much every meditator. When agitation happens, you can try a few remedies and see which are effective for you. For instance, you can relax your body and lower your gaze. If the room is bright, try dimming the lights or pulling some curtains or blinds. You can try wrapping your legs or whole body in a shawl or blanket. You can also take a short break, do some gentle stretching, like a forward bend, and try the practice again.

When you feel dullness you can sit up a little straighter, open your eyes, and raise your gaze. You can remove layers of clothing, open a window to let in fresh air, and brighten the lights if possible. You can also take a short break, stand up, and shake your body, maybe walk around for a few minutes, and then try meditating again.

The Practice: Training in Mindfulness

✦ · · ✦ · · ✦

Mindfulness of body

Find a comfortable posture (on the floor, on a chair, or lying down) with your spine straight but your body loose and relaxed. Begin by relaxing the mind and being simply present for a few moments. Practice dropping awareness into the body and just being in the body for a few minutes. Feel the groundedness of the body, the seeming solidity of the body. When you feel some degree of being rooted in your body in a calm and relaxed way, allow your awareness to notice the natural clarity of the mind. Try to stay grounded in the body while being aware of clarity. Your eyes can be open or closed. Try to notice the state of being calm and clear, relaxed and alert, at the same time. Allow mindfulness to gently return to the groundedness of the body whenever you notice your mind has drifted off into distraction. Adjust your mindfulness if you feel your calmness is too dull, or your clarity is too agitated. Use the principle of *short moments, many times*.

Mindfulness of sensations and feelings

Begin as before, by dropping into the body and relaxing for a little while. Allow mindful awareness to encompass the world of sensations and feelings. This can include physical sensations of warmth and coolness and so on, and feelings of tightness, looseness, excitement, and so on. You are not looking for particular sensations or feelings, just being mindful and aware of whatever is happening. While continuing to relax and settle into sensations and feelings, notice the natural clarity that lets you experience the feeling world. Allow mindful awareness to be relaxed and alert at the same time. When the mind wanders into distraction, use mindfulness of sensations and feelings to gently bring it back. Again, use the principle of *short moments, many times*.

Mindfulness of thoughts and emotions

Again, begin by dropping into the body and relaxing for a little while. Now allow mindful awareness to notice the arising and dissolving of thoughts and emotions. Usually, thoughts and emotions will carry us off into a whole string of secondary thoughts and reactions. Try to remain fresh and present with the thoughts as they arise, without getting involved. It's a delicate balance to watch thoughts and emotions without being sucked into them. They just come and go, and we stay aware of them without reacting. Whenever the mind gets distracted, gently use mindfulness to bring it back. Try to be simple—just be aware of thoughts and emotions in the present moment for short periods. If strong judgments or reactions come up that are so "sticky" they interfere with this practice, handshake for a while.

Handshake by holding the judgments or reactions in open, accepting awareness, without resisting, suppressing, indulging, or ignoring. Just be with the emotions and reactions for a while without any agenda. Alternating handshake practice with mindfulness practice can be very helpful.

✦

As our mindful awareness becomes stronger, thoughts and emotions can become helpers for our practice, rather than obstacles. Early on, we often think a "good" meditation is just peaceful, an absence of disturbing thoughts and emotions. Over time, however, we realize that this notion of peace is limited. We come to understand that thoughts and emotions are like clouds moving across the sky of awareness, and resisting them is what disturbs the mind. A deeper peace is found within the skylike awareness itself, one that isn't bothered whether there are thoughts or emotions or not. At this point, thoughts and emotions emerge as helpers—we aren't bothered by them and we can learn from them.

Settling and Focusing

Begin by dropping into the body and relaxing for a little while. Allow mindful awareness to settle on breathing as its object. Start with a long, deep breath in and a long, deep breath out, just to clear the airways. Now breathe naturally and normally, no need to control the breath. Follow the in breath all the way from outside the body through the nostrils, down the throat, and into the lungs. Feel the sensations of the breath all along the way. Notice how the body feels when the breath is fully inside. Follow the out breath from the lungs, up through the throat, out the nostrils, and into space. Notice the sensations all along the way. Notice how the body feels when the breath is fully outside. Allow mindful awareness to relax as it follows the breath in and out of the body. Try to remain balanced— not too tight and not too loose. Allow your mindfulness to follow the breath while your awareness notices the mind itself, as it settles into being calm and clear, relaxed and alert. Use the principle of *short moments, many times.*

Settling without support

Begin as before by dropping into the body and relaxing for a little while. Connect with the calmness and the relaxed quality of awareness. Now gently open your eyes and notice the natural clarity of the mind. Allow your gaze to be soft and open, not staring or focusing on any one object in the visual field. Without focusing on any object in particular, try to settle into nowness, the present moment. Various sensations, thoughts, and perceptions will come and go in the present moment. Just be aware of the coming and going, without getting involved, without reacting. Allow these shifting impressions to be like clouds moving across the sky. Try to establish the view of clear, thought-free nowness. At first, it will last only a few moments at a time, and then the mind will get distracted. When you notice you're distracted, just gently bring the mind back to nowness. Freshness is especially important in this practice. Embrace the short moments, many times. Just be simple—calm and clear, relaxed and alert, and present in nowness. Notice the panoramic quality of awareness— relaxed openness, clear, and naturally settled.

DANIEL GOLEMAN: THE SCIENCE

I'd been a meditator for many years, and I fully expected to have fewer and fewer thoughts intrude during my meditation as time went on. But thoughts just kept coming into my mind.

There they were, every time. *Maybe I'm just no good at this*, I thought. Then came a moment of mindfulness—actually, more like, *Dang! Another thought!*

But then I began to study in the meditative tradition that Tsoknyi Rinpoche practices, and I was reminded that it's not the thoughts themselves that matter but our *relationship* to them. While mindful we can let thoughts go without getting swept up in them.

One of the biggest helps for me with this shift in how I viewed thoughts was when Tsoknyi Rinpoche said, "Keep mindfulness on guard!"

That admonition is a line from a spontaneous poem by the first one to have the name Tsoknyi Rinpoche, the founder of his lineage. And that advice, I realized, has applied from the very beginnings of my meditation practice decades ago to the present.

When I started meditating back in my college days I used a mantra as the focus on my practice. My mind would inevitably wander off on some train of thought or another, and eventually I'd notice it had wandered and I'd bring my focus back to the mantra. Each time I noticed my mind had wandered represented a moment of mindfulness. That kind of mindfulness was a by-the-way, an aid to keeping a one-pointed focus on the mantra.

When I later learned Theravadan-style insight meditation,

mindfulness was an explicit part of the practice. I'd be watching my breath just as before, when I was focusing on the mantra, and when my mind wandered off—and I noticed it had wandered—I'd bring my attention back to the breath. That was the main instruction at the start. And, again, this was a moment of mindfulness.

At a later stage, the insight instruction I followed was to let any thought or feeling come and go without getting swept away by it. Here mindfulness was on guard to notice times my mind would get swept away in some stream of thought.

Then, still later, I turned to Tibetan-style practice—at first with Tsoknyi's father, Tulku Urgyen Rinpoche, then, after he passed away, with his sons Chokyi Nyima, Chokling, Mingyur (all Rinpoches), and, of course, Tsoknyi Rinpoche. Here mindfulness transforms into something a bit different. Instead of making some extra effort to be mindful, this scanning emerges from resting in awareness itself.

The scientific findings on each of these meditation practices continue to be quite robust, though they were meager way back in the 1970s when I started out doing research on how meditation helps us recover from stress. These days there are more than a thousand peer-reviewed articles published on meditation in general (and mindfulness in particular) each year. Recently, with my old friend neuroscientist Richard Davidson from the University of Wisconsin, I coauthored a book summarizing the best of this research.

Mindfulness of the breath, we found, seems the method most frequently studied by researchers. Sound research has established a long list of benefits from this simple method, tuning into the natural flow of your in breath and out breath, merely observing its sensations without trying to control your breathing in any way.

The strongest findings, repeated by scientific studies over and over in many different ways, show that simply watching your breath and letting other thoughts come and go (emphasis on *go*) has a deeply relaxing effect. In the Tibetan world, these methods are known as *shamata* or *shiney*; they calm you down.

Science now verifies this calming benefit. People who practice simple mindfulness of the breath, for instance, become more relaxed in their daily lives and recover from upsets more quickly than non-meditators. The method seems to calm the amygdala, so that we are pitched into the fight-or-flight state less often.

And the more time over the years you put into this mindfulness method, the less reactive you become. Troubling events trigger you into an upset state far less often. If you are triggered, your upset is less strong. And—maybe the biggest calming benefit—you recover more quickly than you did formerly. In psychological science the speed with which you recover from upset to calm defines "resilience": the quicker you recover, the more resilient you are.

There are other benefits from being able to keep your focus mindfully on your breath. For instance, research at Stanford University found that if you are focused on an important project and then stop to answer a text or email, and end up browsing the web, when you finally return to your important project your focus has dimmed. It takes you some time to ramp up your concentration to the previous level. Unless you did ten minutes of mindfulness of your breath a couple of times that day—then you have little or no loss of concentration after "multitasking."

Another bonus was found at the University of California, Santa Barbara, when a group of students were randomly assigned to learn mindfulness of the breath. The seniors among them scored considerably better than did those in a control group on their grad school entrance exams. The mindfulness practice seems to have improved their working memory, the aspect of memory crucial for retaining what you learn from studying.

On the other hand, a word of advice from my own experiences to those just starting to do this kind of meditation practice: When they begin meditating many people complain that their mind wanders constantly; some even conclude they can't do the practice at all—their mind is too wild. That's what happened to me.

Actually, this can be a good sign: When we begin to pay attention to our mind's coming and going—that is, first become mindful—we see how distracted our mind usually is. This is a first step in becoming more mindful and in taming the wandering mind. One key is remembering to let go of thoughts as they arise rather than just go along with a train of associations.

Another benefit of meditation—greater clarity—was discovered in a group who were doing six or more hours a day of practice in a three-month retreat. They were practicing mindfulness of the breath (as well as cultivating states like loving kindness and equanimity). At several points during and after the retreat they went through a test where, in very rapid succession, they saw lines of differing lengths. Their task: press a button when they saw a line that was shorter than the others (about one in ten was shorter).

The challenge here turns out to be stopping yourself from a knee-jerk impulse to press the button for short when actually you just saw a long line. But as the retreat went on, the meditators got better and better at this rather mundane impulse inhibition. And this resistance to whim went along with the sense of lessened anxiety, an overall well-being, and recovering more quickly from upsets. Perhaps most telling, these improvements lasted months after the retreat ended.

There's a "dose response" dynamic here: the more you do, the greater the benefits. This has been shown scientifically in several ways. For instance, seasoned *vipassana*, or insight, meditators did one full day of meditation and then the next day underwent a lab test of stress. When stressed the meditators showed a smaller rise in cortisol, a key stress hormone, than did a comparison group who did not meditate.

And when these same seasoned meditators had their brains scanned while they saw disturbing images—e.g., a burn victim—they had a lower level of reactivity in the amygdala. That lessened reactivity was due to a stronger connection between the amygdala and the prefrontal cortex, which manages emotional reactions.

People who had done only the beginning practice, mindfulness of breathing, did not show the strengthened connection, or lessened reactivity. But continued practice seems to enhance this connection and lower emotional reactivity to stress. When the most and least experienced among the seasoned meditators were compared, the more hours of lifetime practice, the faster the amygdala recovered from stress.

Then there's a finding that defied the predictions of experts in DNA research. Genomic scientists thought that changes in our DNA could occur because of impacts from our environment, even diet, but not due to a mental exercise like meditation. Wrong.

The finding that meditation has an active impact on our genes was, before the study was done, dismissed as a naive idea by one genomic expert. But then the Davidson group had long-term meditators do a full day of meditation, and examined their genetic activity before that day and afterward.

A bit of background. You may know that it isn't the genes our body carries that determine what happens to us biologically but rather whether they turn on—that is, "express" themselves, in the language of gene specialists. The genes targeted in this study were all responsible for aspects of the body's inflammatory response. When such genes are active over the years, we are prone to diseases like arthritis, diabetes, cardiovascular troubles, and a host of other illnesses where chronic low-grade inflammation contributes to the causes.

We're better off if we can "downregulate" those inflammatory genes—that is, turn them off. That's exactly what the Davidson group found after eight hours of meditation in these long-term *vipassana* practitioners (their average lifetime hours of practice was in the range of six thousand). This "naive" idea turned out to be true.

Several other studies have suggested beneficial effects from meditation on our genes. Beginners in mindfulness, for instance, showed lowered levels of inflammatory gene activity, as well as lessened feelings of loneliness. Feeling lonely, it turns out, boosts the activity of these genes, making the body more a victim of inflammation.

So if people in your life say you're wasting your time meditating when you could be getting something useful done, tell them you are doing a mental workout. It's like going to the gym but for your mind.

EIGHT

· —— · ✦ · —— ·

A DEEPER LOOK WITHIN

TSOKNYI RINPOCHE: THE EXPLANATION

As our mind settles with clarity and we find we can do so more and more often, we might think that this is the end of our path—*I've got what I wanted from meditation.* It's true that we have gotten something valuable: our mind has gone from being turbulent and scattered to being more calm and clear. But actually we have only begun to open our mind's inner potential. Just as we can use essence love to heal our feeling worlds and make our relationships healthy, we can use being more calm and clear to sharpen our insight through the practice called *vipassana*, which means "superior vision" or "inquiry." This practice is a rich and beloved tradition across all forms of Buddhism.

Calmness and insight work together in this inner inquiry. When it comes to the transformative capacity of calmness and insight, we can use an analogy—of trimming weeds versus pulling them completely out of the ground. Calmness is like trimming them back. Insight is like pulling them completely out, roots and all. A temporary state of calmness (trimming the weeds) is fragile because given the right conditions our minds can be thrown into confusion, turmoil, and afflictive emotions again. With calmness, we have found a valuable tool but not addressed the underlying root cause. For that we need deeper understanding.

In my tradition, the key issue in the practice of insight is *understanding reification*—the tendency to make things more concrete or realer than they naturally are. I use *reification* to mean *solidifying*—imputing a solid, fixed reality to things. What do we reify? Everything! When our mind reifies, all we experience gets seen through that lens. Reifying is like believing a dream is real. If we believe our dreams are real, then we can get very excited by sweet dreams and very scared and upset by bad dreams. We do the same during the day, with our memories, thoughts, and fantasies.

We automatically reify our perceptions as we experience an "I" who is subject and what's in the world around us (or in us, as with our thoughts) as object. This habit of reification has become the tendency to fixate deep in our being. The problem here: reification leads to mental and physical tightness. This sets us up for problems like increased anxiety, fear, stubbornness, heaviness, inflexibility, uncontrollable moods, neurotic thinking, and so on. Tightness destroys our joy and playfulness, our flow. Everything becomes a little too serious, a big deal. The more we reify, the harder it is to relax, to laugh at ourselves, to be open. So it's helpful to experience ourselves and our world in less reified ways.

All about Me

In particular we reify our sense of self. Some of my friends are obsessed with food, nature, art, or sports, but in my tradition, we are obsessed with the self. We think about it, study it, meditate on it. You might wonder, *Why are you so obsessed about the self? It's just there, so get over it!* Reifying and clinging to the self in unhealthy ways leads to a lot of needless suffering. But reifying the self is just a habit, a stubborn habit with a long history. The good news is that like any habit, it can be changed.

Each of us, of course, has a unique mind-stream. My body isn't the same as your body. My memories and thoughts aren't the same as your memories and thoughts. The problems start when the reifying tendency fixates on a strong sense of ownership and identification. *Me* and *mine* become very important. People and things are evaluated not for what they are, but for what they can help *me* with, what they can help *me* get. The self becomes a center of a lot of hope and fear, a lot of grasping, a lot of unrealistic expectations—of ourselves and others. Then things become more and more unhealthy. The stronger our self-grasping is, the stronger emotions like anger, jealousy, anxiety, and pride will be.

Our habit of reifying the self is based on a subtle misunderstanding: We impute qualities to the body and mind that aren't actually there. We think there should be some kind of reliable certainty, some kind of lasting stability. We think our body and mind should be independent, not relying on other people and things. For short periods these illusions can persist, and we buy into the illusion. Then we get sick or something tough happens in our life and our mind becomes turbulent again. When the body breaks down or our mind gets stressed, turbulent, or unhappy, they are showing us what they always were—a collection of parts that can fail anytime, like those in a bicycle or a car. As we familiarize ourselves with this inherent uncertainty we will become more resilient, because our understanding will more closely match the reality. When we understand our true nature more accurately, our expectations will be more realistic and healthier.

A common teaching in my tradition is *selflessness*. This term is often misunderstood when people take it too far. It doesn't mean there is no personality, that there isn't a sense of self at all. It's not a voidlike, nihilistic total absence. Cultivating insight about the true nature of the self doesn't make someone into a frozen vegetable, or a cold marble statue. If you ask someone who embodies selflessness, like a Buddha, *Where are you going?*, they wouldn't say, *What does that mean?* That would be ridiculous. A Buddha is highly functional—maybe more functional than we can imagine. A Buddha knows what conventions are and how to use them, and also knows the limitations of conventions and how to transcend them.

Selflessness means that the sense of self we all have isn't solid and truly real. It's shifty, sneaky, and dreamlike. When we search within for our self we might *feel* something, but that doesn't mean it's a real thing like solid matter. It may seem to us that our self is based on our body and mind. Or maybe we think it's some independent thing like a permanent soul. But when we look for it, when we actually examine our body and mind, we can't quite find it. The body and mind keep changing. They are composed of many, many parts and function in a web of interdependence. The sense of self also keeps changing. It comes and goes. We form and shift and dissolve various identities in response to different situations, such as whom we are with. We can be children and parents, teachers and students, givers and receivers, inflexible and yielding. We can feel vulnerable, empowered, uneasy, or secure, depending on who is reflecting back to us. The sense of self is always in constant flux.

The Four I's

So what is the "self"? The sense of self is a habit that arises and ceases in awareness. The habit is the reification of the sense of an observer, a knower at the center of our experience.

Take the example of a car. On the surface, there is a car. It's right in front of me. I can get in and drive it around. But if you take apart the car, you have a pile of things—doors, engine, axles, wheels, tires, and so on. Where then is the "car"? The "car" reveals itself as an abstraction, an imputation to a collection of parts. The self is like this, a label that usefully describes a conceptual "entity" composed of many parts. In the case of the self, the parts are the body, sensations, perceptions, mental formations, and consciousness.

There are many ways in my tradition to talk and think about

the self. I like to use a simple framework called *the four I's.* This framework comes from many different sources, which I've brought together and given unifying names. These four I's can help us get more clarity on how the sense of self operates in both healthy and unhealthy ways.

The Mere I

So if the sense of self is shifty, sneaky, dreamlike, changeable, and interdependent, what is the appropriate way to relate to it? With a sense of *mereness. Mereness* is the opposite of reification. It's a light touch, an appropriate quality of holding. If you need to hold a piece of tissue paper, clamping down hard and squeezing is too much. Just hold it lightly. The sense of self merely seems to be here. Objects of experience merely seem to be there. The sense of self merely experiences various sense perceptions and thoughts. It merely remembers and plans for the future. It merely feels like I am here—we do not need to fixate on it. Dreams merely appear without being solid and real. Reflections and mirages merely appear. The *mere I* is the healthy way to relate to the sense of self, and to our changing experiences. With mereness, we can move with reality, we can dance and flow. We are in harmony with the natural reality rather than out of harmony.

The truth is everything is moving and changing. If we know this we can find some openness, flexibility, and fluidity that will ease reification. And then some insight might dawn into interconnectedness: All things depend on other things. When we see the body and mind are not a oneness but rather are collections of parts, we open to fluidity and multiplicity. We can allow more experiences to freely come and freely go, without needing to form a narrative and reconcile them with who we thought we were.

Sometimes I call this the *beautiful, functional* mere I. It's beautiful because it is responsive instead of reactive. It is light and playful, ready to love, but not in a sticky way. It is flexible and simple; it has basic okayness. It isn't dominated by hidden secret agendas of reifying and self-cherishing. The mere I is a true home for a healthy human being, like groundedness and essence love. To connect with the mere I we have to learn to let go. The mere I is a way of being we can come back to, to find sanity, release tension, and connect with openness.

The Reified I

When the mereness is not recognized, reification sneaks in. The sense of self becomes more concrete, like a very solid thing. I call this the *reified I*. The apparent separation between ourselves and our experience, the experiencer and our perceptions, becomes rigid and distinct.

Instead of observing, *It feels a little uneasy and anxious in my body this morning. Hmm, maybe it's a weird mood. Let's see how it develops*, we concretize our perceptions: "Today is an awful day! This situation is terrible! Everyone is against me!"

Our world is splitting more and more, *self and other, in here and out there*. We keep reifying and the whole thing becomes very uptight. Instead of seeing the interdependent play of everything, the mereness, we lose that beauty and fluidity, and keep tightening inside. As this hardens more and more, we can lose our intrinsic joy, our intrinsic well-being. Eventually it creates a self-centeredness.

The reified I has coarse and subtle dimensions. In its coarse sense, it bites and clinches down on all sorts of things. It makes situations and relationships tight, heavy, and serious. Imagine clenching your teeth and furrowing your brow. That gesture exaggerates but exemplifies the reified I's attitude. In its subtle dimensions, it just believes in things a little too much. Instead of relating to the passing flow of experience with looseness, joy, and playfulness, it concretizes and fixates. It makes smiles a little tighter, it makes it a little harder to laugh. The reified I solidifies our successes and struggles, our highs and lows.

A common misunderstanding is thinking that without reification, nothing can function. This is an important point to clarify. We might think, *I need seriousness. Without a very serious, self-oriented manner, I cannot do anything.* But reality is not fixed. When we try to pin everything down there is no dance, no flow, no movement. We might know this intellectually, but we have learned early in life that to feel safe emotionally we like things to be fixed. Slowly the fixing becomes too much, bringing us extra suffering. Even when we know we need to let go, we don't know how. This is because of fixation, the reified I.

The Needy I

The *needy I* develops out of the reified I as we grow more self-centered and self-cherishing. The needy I is easier to see than the mere I or the reified I; we can see it in what we normally consider to be selfish or needy behavior. By missing the mereness, we've lost touch with our basic groundedness, openness, and freedom, our fluidity and playfulness. Our reified I is uptight, not joyful and playful. We might sense something is missing, but we try to remedy it in the wrong way. Instead of seeing that the reified I itself is problematic, we mistakenly think our reified I is lacking something, and so we try to find and consume that, whether it's love, acceptance, possessions, status, or whatever. We become cherishers of ourselves, of our fragile egos. The self-cherishing I essentially involves claiming happiness only for myself.

In reality, happiness exists interdependently. This means we have to take care of others' well-being. But when we are manifesting the self-cherishing I, we feel the urge for happiness for ourselves—and that cannot be achieved, because our happiness depends on that of others. When everything is all about me, we become very lonely. A key sign of the self-cherishing I is the selfish search for happiness for only myself.

The Social I

The *social I* entails the understanding that we have a certain existence in other people's perceptions. Others have mental images of us, evaluate us, form opinions of us, and judge us. We can be liked or disliked, become popular or unpopular. The social I is our understanding of this, our anxieties or playfulness about it, and our attempts to manage it. We all have to deal with it, unless we live alone in the mountains. The social I is not inherently positive or negative. The social I can express the mere I or the reified and needy I. When the mere I is behind it the social I can be very useful, if we know how to play with it. The social I can be very fun, when we're playing with humor and the mere I. Without the influence and agendas of the self-cherishing I, the social I can be suffused with a sense of altruism and compassion. Then the social I can help many people.

I like to think of the Dalai Lama as an example of a very healthy social I. Of course the Dalai Lama has a developed social I. He functions at a high level and uses his social I of "the Dalai Lama" most of the day, all over the world, and with many, many people. Despite this, the Dalai Lama often says he doesn't dream of being a hugely famous lama. He dreams of himself as a simple monk. This shows his social I is based on the mere I instead of the reified I. When he goes back to his room, he can let the social I dissolve and come back to the mere I, which is very simple, very healthy. He isn't stuck in the reified I. The Dalai Lama sets a very high standard, one we may not attain just now. But it is helpful to have an example, a goal to orient toward.

On the other hand, when the reified I develops into the self-cherishing I, then our social I goes wrong. We want recognition, popularity, acclaim, fame, and so on. We start to worry about our reputation. The management of our social I can be exhausting and lead to a lot of anxiety. These days, I'm concerned about how social media can make the social I even more stressful than before. It affects all of us, but especially younger people, who spend a lot of time in that world.

Permanence, Singularity and Independence

Generally, we often have the sense that our self has permanence, that it's a singular and unified entity, and that our self is independent. Our habit of reification—the root of confusion—stems from these core assumptions. We impute qualities to our sense of self and to the objects of our perceptions that aren't actually there.

Permanence might sound somehow grand and strange—we know in the back of our minds that somehow things aren't actually endless. Yet we forget our bodies are constantly changing, our minds are constantly changing, our mood is changing. Everything is in a flow, in transition. The basic building blocks of mind and matter are constantly arising and ceasing, appearing and vanishing, being born and passing way. Reality is more like a sparkling river than a collection of dead objects sitting in space. Emotionally, when we forget about this constant flux, our moods carry great weight. *I am this mood. I will always be like this.* So, for instance, when things don't go our way, we can feel like our world is ending.

But by staying in touch with flux we can have perspective, we can remember, *This too shall pass*. By internalizing the realization of constant change, we can stay grounded with the ups and downs.

Taking things as *singular* means thinking that a collection of many parts is one thing. I like to call it *lumping*—we think the body is a lump, the self is a lump, objects we perceive are lumps. This lumping creates various problems. For example, the body, feelings, mind, and the sense of self are actually distinct streams of experience. But we often lump them together into "me." Then when one of them isn't feeling very good, it seems like a problem for all of them. We lose the space among them, around them. We feel more stuck. Another problem is we can lump together other people and their emotions. When someone has an emotion, we think, *They are that emotion*, rather than understanding that emotion is temporarily dominating them. Then we can blame them for their emotions, thinking, *This is a bad person*, and hold grudges and biases, based on something temporary that is not intrinsic to their being.

Finally, there is *independence*. We all like the idea of independence. It sounds good as an ideal. We impute independence to our sense of self—*I'm independent; I don't need anyone!* We feel proud, but this quickly becomes a lonely pride. It's confusion, not based in reality. We also impute independence to objects of our perceptions, including other people, thinking they have the freedom to control their body, speech, and mind. But in reality, nothing is really independent, including our sense of self. Things are interdependent; everything depends on other things. The tree depends on rain, air, soil, sunlight, and insects for pollination. Our bodies depend on food, water, air, and so many other things to survive. If we want to thrive, we depend on even more conditions. Everything is connected to so many things.

Flux, Multiplicity, and Interconnectedness

The root of confusion is fixation, and the basis of fixation is confusion. It need not be like that. Our sense of self and the objects we're perceiving can be playful. Joy will come out of playfulness. This accords with nature. Everything is playing—trees, wind, mountains. Everything is interdependently playing, not grasping, not reifying.

So we have to relax, and find space and openness. The opposites of the misunderstandings previously described are *flux*, *multiplicity*, and *interconnectedness*. Once we've contemplated these and resolved them, we can bring them to mind again and again to help bring perspective in daily life. We can remember interconnectedness and interdependency. We can come back to the beautiful mere I. The simple, beautiful mere I. Due to interconnectedness, there is the possibility of loving everyone, because we are depending on everyone.

The Practice

Now we need to bring all the previous practices we've learned and integrate them with the understanding of the mere I, without reification. We can learn how to drop into the mere I. When we see solidity, the self-cherishing appearing, we can drop into the body and find essence love. We can experience essence love with the open, beautiful mere I, without grasping. We can handshake without reification. We can work with our speedy energy and find groundedness with the mere I. We can practice settling the mind and finding clarity without reification. This understanding of mereness, of not fixating, can pervade everything we practice, everything we perceive.

Also, don't reify your meditation practice. We can tighten up around our precious meditation, but this just brings old habits of tension, judgment, and ambition into our spiritual path. Meditation can rather be an arena to challenge the habits of reification, fixation, and tightness. Our spiritual path can be a refuge to foster playfulness, joy, openness, and love.

The main practice, then, is to come back to the mere I. If we understand the four I's in our experience, then we can realize, *Oh, now I'm in the reified, the social, or the self-cherishing I.* We need to identify these in experience. The coming back to the mere I is a combination of understanding where we're stuck and letting go.

◆ · · ◆ · · ◆

Begin by taking a comfortable posture, with your spine straight and body and mind relaxed. Prepare for insight practice by dropping into the body for a few minutes. Connect with the feeling world. If you feel something needs a handshake, do that practice. If you can connect with essence love, allow it to suffuse your heart and body. Now allow the mind to settle into calmness and clarity for a little while. When you feel sufficiently calm and clear, try to be aware of which I is operating in this moment. Know it, feel it, clearly identify it.

Try to come back to the mere I. Use your understanding of impermanence, interdependence, and multiplicity. Things may seem obstructive and oppressive, tight and serious, but these themselves are shifting perceptions. Use your practice of letting go. Whatever the weather may be, the sky remains open and accommodating. Keep finding the points of tension and tightness in the body, feeling world and mind, and releasing them.

Use your handshake and your essence love. When beautiful monsters appear, our difficult emotions and resistance, welcome them with the open hand of accepting awareness. Reconnect again and again with essence love, until it feels like your home, your ground. If you can come back to the mere I, just stay there and be with that. If you can't drop and come back to the mere I, relax your efforts and handshake whatever is present.

◆

Sometimes the reified I seems quite strong, and it's hard to let go in the mere I. If you find that's the case with you, then you can try this:

Begin as before, by taking a comfortable posture and dropping awareness into the body. Just be in the body and feeling world for a little while, with no agenda. Allow your awareness to settle into grounded calm and clarity. When you feel centered and balanced, try to bring attention to the reified I. Try to find the solidity, the tightness of the reified I. You may notice it as a subtle underlying gripping, a seriousness. If you can find it, allow yourself to feel it for a while to get to know it better. After some time, try to smile inwardly and remember the mereness. Try to relax and loosen the grip of the reified I. Drop into the mere I. If you cannot drop the reified I, practice handshake at this point.

We can practice in our daily life too:

Again, the essential practice is coming back to the mere I. No matter what else you are doing, try to remember the key points of understanding, letting go, just being with the present experience, and handshaking the feeling world. Whenever possible, connect with essence love. Allow essence love to permeate the mere I, and the mereness to permeate essence love.

Having connected with essence love and the mere I, if you need to engage with the social I, if you need to play a role with particular people, play it. Engage with it. Whether with others or alone, remember everything is moving and changing, everything is interconnected. When the reified I causes problems, no need to panic. Just observe it, clearly identify it, and learn from it. With understanding, anything can be brought onto your path of meditation and wisdom.

In response to any situation you encounter, apply whichever practice is appropriate. Dropping, handshake, essence love, breathing, settling, or finding clarity, bring whichever is helpful at any time, without reification. Whenever possible, drop back into the mere I. Try to integrate groundedness, essence love, and the mere I in your experience, so they become your home, your ground. Allow the beauty of mereness to touch all your spiritual practices, every part of you, everything you perceive, and all beings you connect with.

DANIEL GOLEMAN: THE SCIENCE

Tulku Urgyen, Tsoknyi Rinpoche's father, was one of the most revered meditation masters of his time. My wife and I were fortunate enough to meet with him a few times, for several weeks at a stretch, before he passed away in 1996.

While his loving presence was palpable, I was struck by another quality: his humility. Whenever he would teach about a Tibetan text, he would first acknowledge his own teacher from whom he received this particular instruction.

Then he would always state a disclaimer, one that went, in effect, like this: "I don't have any particular accomplishments, but I'll do my best based on what my teachers have told me."

This humble attitude stands in stark contrast to the me-first, ego-feeding style so common—even admired—in modern culture. In Tsoknyi Rinpoche's model of our various selves, Tulku Urgyen's attitude voiced the mere I, which has not the least need to impress others or pump itself up.

When Richard Davidson and I surveyed all the best research to date on meditation—out of thousands such studies published—we discovered a remarkable gap. There were countless findings on such popular benefits of meditation as becoming more calm and more focused, relaxation, better health, and other such payoffs. But there was very little research on how pursuing meditation lessens our ego-grasping, and virtually zero on selflessness—the mere I, as Tsoknyi calls it.

He sees this as the healthiest "I," where we hold our sense of self lightly, as we do every other thought or emotion. We recognize our uniqueness and whatever value there may be in, say, our social I—but see it all as a mere display, like a reflection in a mirror. We can be playful or serious as the moment calls for, because we are not limited by neediness or the need to defend some sense of ourselves. We are completely available to the needs of the other person.

But this model of an ultra-healthy self hinges on a lightness of being that has no parallel in modern psychology. It's our ordinary stream of me-focused consciousness, with its endless worries, desires and concerns, hopes and fears, to-do lists and the like, that weighs us down. This frothy mental concoction builds what we think of as our "self"—the stuff of being "me." This sense of self gives us a feeling of home within the shifting ocean of our experience.

But traditional Asian psychologies take a different view: as Vasubandhu, an Indian sage, noted way back in the fifth century, "So long as you grasp at the self, you stay bound to the world of suffering." Freedom from our ordinary self—and resting in the mere I—has always been a goal of Asian spiritual paths.

The nature of "suffering" in our ordinary lives can be elusive for most of us. Yet many of the experiences that spiritual paths see as our suffering can sometimes look like it to one and all. Take the relationship between depression and the reified I, where thoughts and feelings are "stickiest." Hallmarks of depression include an intense self-focus and persistent, repetitive brooding. Such clinging to our thoughts and ruminating on them over and over has been identified as one of the mechanisms driving depression. Thoughts like *I'm a failure* and *My life is pointless* are what's called "depressionogenic"—that is, they spur bouts of depression.

The most successful psychotherapies for depression encourage people to see such thoughts in a new way: changing one's relationship to them rather than simply believing them. Indeed, one of the maxims in this kind of psychotherapy is that "you don't have to believe your thoughts," particularly the ones that make you depressed. Sometimes called "decentering," this shift in relationship to negative thoughts marks a point where psychotherapy and meditation—especially mindfulness—meet.

The needy I, like the reified I, also seems to reflect the activity of the brain's emotional circuits. Here a sticky self-centeredness makes the preoccupation with our sense of self—I, me, mine— thickest. Our mind fixates on what rewards us and avoids what's unpleasant. This can lead to narcissistic focus on what we want without regard for how that might impact other people, or to unhealthy relationship patterns like a needy dependence.

How our childhood attachments shape relationships throughout our adult life has been analyzed to a great extent in work that stems from British child expert John Bowlby's theories. A childhood where we feel neglect, or even trauma, for instance, leads to a sense of mistrust in our adult relationships. Similarly, if our childhood led us to seek attention by overreacting or becoming ultra-anxious about connections, we take that stance in adult years. Or if we handled our anxieties about connection in childhood by tuning out of all emotion, that's what we do as adults. But if our earliest years made us feel secure with people, we carry that presumption of safety with us into our closest relationships.

Then there's the social I, the way we exist in other people's minds. Some people put great energy into what psychology calls "impression management," trying to manipulate how we are seen—no matter who and how we really are underneath. The negative side of the social I comes from wanting to be liked, at any cost—including projecting a false self. Social media puts the social I on steroids, as, for instance, people desperately try to increase engagement from their followers.

On the other hand, the social I can be quite positive when we realize its potential and are motivated by a sense of caring, not by neediness. As Tsoknyi Rinpoche points out, the Dalai Lama exemplifies this; he's become a spokesperson for the oneness of humanity and the need for a guiding ethic based on compassion. When Paul Ekman, a world expert on the facial expression of emotion, met the Dalai Lama, he was immediately impressed by the famous monk's emotional agility. As the Dalai Lama met people, one after another, Ekman saw the monk's face would instantly mirror the emotions of the person he was greeting—and then vanish as his face mirrored that of the next person.

Ekman had never seen such rapid, seamless transition from intense sadness, for instance, to powerful joy. That shift seems to indicate a lack of "stickiness." As we free ourselves from distressing emotions and compulsive wants, we can draw nearer to what Ekman saw in the Dalai Lama—being unstuck—that is, the mere I. We go from a rigid sense of self to a more flexible, in-the-moment way of manifesting.

Neuroscience tells us the thickest sense of self occurs when we are "doing nothing"—that is, when the mind wanders here and there. Mostly that wandering entails thoughts about ourselves: *what worries me, how many likes I got on my post, my relationships, my emotion of the moment*. The swath of brain circuitry active during these idle moments of me-focused reverie is called the *default mode network*, a name that indicates this circuitry takes over by default when we are not engaged in, say something that requires we focus on the mental task at hand, like, say, solving an arithmetic problem.

The self-system creates our personal universe by putting every event in terms of how it affects us; we are always the center of the stories we tell ourselves about life. And while we do so, the default mode network activates. But long-term meditators, research finds, have strengthened brain circuits that quiet the default mode.

What research exists tracking progress in meditation against the strength of the brain's self-system, Davidson and I found, indicates that the longer someone has been a meditator, the less strong connections become in that system for creating the self. This may track the ability of a meditator to simply notice an experience (an aching knee, say) and letting it pass rather than being caught by it. The mere I can more readily do this, while the reified I gets caught by the urge to do something to avoid the pain.

Cognitive science has determined that what we take to be our solid "self" actually is constructed from bits and pieces of perceptions, memories, thoughts, and other such mental ephemera. The brain maintains this sense of an ongoing self from a mélange of passing phenomena. It's an illusion, constantly built for us over and over by our brain—so much for the permanent I. One of the major insights of Buddhism parallels this understanding when it tells us there is no self as such—just the illusion of a self.

Psychology, for example, studies the kind of humility masters like Tulku Urgyen displayed, though in less pleasing terms: the technical term is *hypo-egoic nonentitlement*. That might translate into something like "egoless non-specialness"—that is, "not feeling special," an attitude the exact opposite of narcissism.

Neuroscience has, at least in theory, begun to track what the mere I might mean in terms of brain function. Here the science remains speculative; there are no studies to date of the brain's wiring for creating a sense of self and how that changes as we become more familiar with the mere I. One theory suggests that "deconstructive meditation"—that is, practices that bring us closer to the experience of the mere I, where we are less and less in the sway of the reified or self-cherishing I, entail sustaining a state of pure awareness.

The science goes a step further, suggesting what this state of pure awareness might mean in terms of brain function. This view sees the brain as continually making predictions based on our past experience, sometimes called "proflection." But the closer we get to resting our awareness in the present moment, the less strongly we anticipate the future at all, let alone as based on our past. As we are able to sustain this present-moment awareness devoid of past and future, the brain circuitry for ordinary awareness quiets—at least that's the speculation.

The benefits of quieting the mind include becoming more calm and clear. But resting in pure awareness goes a step beyond this sense of quiet. Richard Davidson, who studied the brains of highly advanced yogis who had attained this level, tells me that he had never met any group of people so present, joyous, and warm-hearted.

EPILOGUE: SOME FINAL ADVICE

· —— · ✦ · —— ·

GROUNDED BODY, OPEN HEART, CLEAR MIND

Our vision with this book is to help create healthy people, in every sense: grounded, warmhearted, clear-minded people, who have the energy and natural inclination to help others. A simple slogan captures this vision: *grounded body, open heart, clear mind.* This expresses the result of training in the many practices we've offered here.

As we become more adept at using these tools, we can apply the right one for a given situation, like a skilled carpenter who knows what tool to use for each part of a project. Our lives present us with obstacles, challenges, and problems, whether in our relationships or inside, in our internal world of feelings, thoughts, and emotions. We can think of these methods as a toolbox for dealing with life:

DROPPING: When you feel tense, uptight, stuck, or anxious, dropping practice can be very helpful. You coordinate a big breath out with slapping your hands on your thighs and dropping the thinking mind and landing in the body. You can use this quick-and-easy practice as needed throughout the day.

BELLY-BREATHING: Belly-breathing can be particularly useful when you feel speedy and ungrounded. This multistep breathing practice helps you bring speedy energy down to its home below the navel, grounding you.

HANDSHAKE: This essential tool for healing and opening helps with emotional blockages, reactivity, and resistance— your "beautiful monsters." You reconnect your awareness and your feeling world with an attitude of welcoming and acceptance, befriending your beautiful monsters.

ESSENCE LOVE: The handshake with your feeling world lets you rediscover the natural well-being that comes from connecting with essence love. When you feel needy, dry, unworthy, uninspired, or underappreciated you can first handshake these feelings and befriend them, which, over time, lets you reconnect with your intrinsic okayness, essence love. Essence love is always with us, underneath all our changing feelings, emotions, and moods.

LOVE AND COMPASSION: Rooted in essence love, you can cultivate empathy and compassion anytime, gradually expanding their scope to hold more and more beings in your tender caring. This can expand to include neutral and difficult people, not just people who are already close to our hearts.

SETTLING THE MIND: When you feel scattered, unfocused, or confused, the settling-the-mind practices can help. Learning to settle the mind with an object of support, such as the breath, and without an object of support are both important practices to discover natural clarity and bring calmness and focus into your life.

INSIGHT PRACTICE: The practices of insight, including focused contemplation on the four I's and resting in lucid spaciousness, can deepen your spiritual path and unlock liberating insight. Insight practice clarifies healthy and unhealthy ways of relating to the self, helping you develop more robust calmness and lucidity and discover your potential for freedom from neuroses, limiting beliefs, and confusion.

These practices and their resulting insights can help us deal with life and its messiness more gracefully and effectively. The key points are *groundedness* from dropping, *essence love* from handshake, and the *mere I* from insight. These can become our inner home, our ground of being. If we're able to do that, life can become richer, warmer, more joyful, and we will be able to help others more easily.

But as with any skill, we need to practice these. If we want to get good at the piano, at woodworking, at a sport or a hobby, we have to repeat the key movements many, many times, until we become proficient. It's the same with the mind. We can't meditate once or twice and get all the benefits and skills that meditation can offer. It takes some time. We have to *familiarize* ourselves with the practices and the experiences that happen when we do them. In fact, the traditional Tibetan word for meditation—*gom*—actually means familiarizing or habituating. We are counteracting old habits and creating new habits.

Ideally we'd devote some time every day. It doesn't have to be a long stretch; it's better to set achievable goals, like ten to twenty minutes per day, to start. This is enough to get some benefits right away, and then gradually increase the time. It's better to let our practice grow organically than trying to force ourselves too much in the beginning. You can try starting with a month pledge—to meditate every day for a month—to help get you off the ground and create the habit.

Remember that meditation experiences keep rising and falling, like our moods or the stock market. Sometimes we feel clear, light, and elated, like we're making rapid progress. Other times we feel sluggish or agitated, like we're not getting anywhere, like anything but meditation would be better. Just keep going without getting too caught up in our shifting experiences. *It doesn't really matter what our changing experiences are*, so long as we keep practicing and developing these habits. In the end, our experiences are like waves in the ocean, but despite their ups and downs, what matters is that we're still in the water.

Crests and troughs are both just the water in the ocean, and highs and lows in our ever-changing experience are both just the flow of awareness. Don't judge them. That can end up puffing up our egos or deflating us. If we want to reach a high mountaintop, we just have to keep steadily walking—our mood at any particular moment is not so important.

There are many ways of helping others, but this path of meditation we encourage emphasizes beginning with your own being. By helping yourself you help others. First come home and develop inner strength; your path of meditation takes you to essence love and, as you cultivate clarity and inner richness, then expression love will dawn as compassion. Helping others makes a huge difference in our world. These practices can help us help ourselves, and then become better able to help others.

Of course helping others—and life in general—can be exhausting. Stress is rampant in the modern world and it takes a toll. The pace of modern life can make us speedy, and the complex demands we have to juggle at home add stresses. The mental, physical, and emotional price can be steep. With these practices we can replenish rather than feel tired, dried-out, and exhausted. We can counteract feeling low energy, and avoid burnout and compassion fatigue. We can learn how to reenergize ourselves. The more energy we have flowing from our practice, the more we can help others. As this positive feedback loop becomes established, we will be able to come back to our natural home, reenergize ourselves, and then keep helping.

For those who help others a lack of self-care can limit their altruistic work, not to mention curb the joy and well-being that can come from helping. If we are not connecting to our hearts, have no meditation, no home in the feeling world, and no clarity, then emotional exhaustion is more likely. But when benevolent work, inner transformation, and self-care combine they can strengthen one another.

As you practice these techniques, compassion and insight will spontaneously dawn—what these methods are designed to produce. An analogy is that once you have fire, you have heat. As you become familiar with these practices you will gradually become a healthier, more genuine person, someone suffused with love, compassion, and wisdom. There are many obstacles in life, but we can learn how to handle them. Anything, positive or negative, can be seen as an opportunity for growth, as a way to strengthen our practice. Therefore, anything can be brought onto the path. Once we know how to handle our problems then we know how to restore ourselves—to energize rather than become exhausted, fed-up, and burned-out. Then we become more like a flower that is blooming into compassionate wisdom.

We sincerely hope this book, and the ideas and practices within, will help many, many people to enjoy their birthright of a grounded body, open heart, and clear mind.

ACKNOWLEDGMENTS

Tsoknyi Rinpoche feels deep gratitude to his root teachers, from whom he received the instructions that evolved into this book. He thanks Adam Kane for his superb effort in helping to write this book. Esteban and Tressa Hollander of Pundarika Foundation gave invaluable help in seeing this project through. Rinpoche adds, "I thank my students, from whom I've learned so much over the years, and my family for their loving support."

Daniel, too, thanks Adam Kane, for giving eloquent voice to Rinpoche's words. Our editor at Simon & Schuster, Stephanie Hitchcock, gave superb guidance every step of the way. And, of course, Daniel thanks his wife, Tara Bennett-Goleman, for her insights, inputs, and warm encouragement of this project.

NOTES

Chapter 2

17 **Research at Stanford University finds:** Sonja Lyubomirsky et al., "Thinking about Rumination: The Scholarly Contributions and Intellectual Legacy of Susan Nolen-Hoeksema," *Annual Review of Clinical Psychology* 11, (March 2015): 1–22, published online January 2, 2015, https://doi.org/10.1146/annurev-clinpsy-032814-112733.

18 **The amygdala is the brain's radar for threat:** Joseph LeDoux, *The Emotional Brain: The Mysterious Underpinnings of Emotional Life* (New York: Simon & Schuster, 1998).

Chapter 3

43 **And such a prolonged, ongoing fight-or-flight reaction:** Bruce McEwen and John Wingfield, "The Concept of Allostasis in Biology and Biomedicine," *Hormones and Behavior* 43, no. 1 (January 2003): 2–15.

44 **This was driven home:** Years later Richard Davidson and I reviewed the most rigorous studies of meditation in our book

Altered Traits: Science Reveals How Meditation Changes Your Brain, Mind, and Body (New York: Penguin Books, 2019).

45 **Dr. Benson was to pursue this finding:** Herbert Benson, *The Relaxation Response*, updated ed. (New York: HarperCollins, updated 2009).

46 **The strictest review of scientific findings:** Andrea Zaccaro et al., "How Breath-Control Can Change Your Life: A Systematic Review on Psycho-Physiological Correlates of Slow Breathing," *Frontiers in Human Neuroscience* 12 (2018): 353, https://www.ncbi.nlm.nih.gov/pmc/articles/PMC6137615/.

47 **One study of slow breathing:** Donald J. Noble and Shawn Hochman, "Hypothesis: Pulmonary Afferent Activity Patterns during Slow, Deep Breathing Contribute to the Neural Induction of Physiological Relaxation," *Frontiers in Physiology* 10 (September 13, 2019): 1176, https://doi.org/10.3389/fphys.2019.0176.

Chapter 4

75 **He was particularly intrigued:** Tara Bennett-Goleman, *Emotional Alchemy: How the Mind Can Heal the Heart* (New York: Harmony Books, 2001).

79 **Volunteers with social anxiety:** Philippe Goldin has conducted a series of brain studies with volunteers who suffer from social anxiety disorder; many of these were done while he was at Stanford University, before going to UC Davis. See, e.g., Philippe R. Goldin et al., "Neural Bases of Social Anxiety Disorder: Emotional Reactivity and Cognitive Regulation during Social and Physical Threat," *Archives of General Psychiatry* 66, no. 2 (February 2009): 170–80.

80 **Chris Gerner:** Chris Gerner studies acceptance in accord with the research on self-compassion of Kristin Neff of the University of Texas at Austin. See, e.g., Kristin Neff and Chris Gerner, *The*

Mindful Self-Compassion Workbook: A Proven Way to Accept Yourself, Build Inner Strength, and Thrive (New York: Guilford Press, 2018).

80 **But research led by Hedy Kober:** Hedy Kober et al., "Let It Be: Mindful Acceptance Down-Regulates Pain and Negative Emotion," *Social Cognitive and Affective Neuroscience* 14, no. 11 (November 1, 2019): 1147–58.

80 **Philippe Goldin's research:** Philippe R. Goldin et al., "Evaluation of Cognitive Behavioral Therapy vs Mindfulness Meditation in Brain Changes during Reappraisal and Acceptance Among Patients with Social Anxiety Disorder: A Randomized Clinical Trial," *JAMA Psychiatry* 78, no.10 (October 1, 2021):1134–42. https://doi.org/10.1001/jamapsychiatry.2021.1862.

Chapter 5

103 **The closest parallel:** See Cortland Dahl et al., "The Plasticity of Well-Being: A Training-Based Framework for the Cultivation of Human Flourishing," *Proceedings of the National Academy of Sciences of the United States of America* 117, no. 51 (December 22, 2020): 32197–206, https://www.doi.org/10.1073/pnas2014859117.

103 **My old friend:** Healthy Mins Innovations, https://hminnovations.org/.

104 **Research at Harvard:** Matthew A. Killingsworth and Daniel T. Gilbert, "A Wandering Mind Is an Unhappy Mind," *Science* 330, no. 6006 (November 2010): 932. DOI: 10.1126/science.1192439.

104 **Critical brain circuits:** Dahl et al., "Plasticity of Well-Being."

105 **When I talked to Richie:** Richard J. Davidson with Sharon Begley, *The Emotional Life of Your Brain: How Its Unique Patterns Affect the Way You Think, Feel, and Live—and How You Can Change Them* (New York: Avery, 2012).

Chapter 6

133 **But it wasn't until 2008:** Antoine Lutz et al., "Regulation of the Neural Circuitry of Emotion by Compassion Meditation: Effects of Meditative Expertise," *PLOS One*, March 26, 2008.

133 **Back in the 1980s:** Dalai Lama, *Worlds in Harmony: Dialogues on Compassionate Action* (Berkeley, CA: Parallax Press, 2004).

134 **Research tells us:** Jean Decety, "The Neurodevelopment of Empathy," *Developmental Neuroscience* 32, no. 4 (December 2010): 257–67.

136 **The trained groups:** Olga Klimecki, "Differential Pattern of Functional Brain Plasticity after Compassion and Empathy Training," *Cerebral Cortex* 23, no. 7 (2013): 1552–61.

137 **Afterward the compassion group:** Helen Y. Weng et al., "Compassion Training Alters Altruism and Neural Responses to Suffering," *Psychological Science* 24, no. 7 (May 2013): published online May 21, 2013, http://pss.sagepub.com/early/2013/05/20 /0956797612469537.

137 **Compared with a group of volunteers:** Julieta Galante et al., "Loving-Kindness Meditation Effects on Well-Being and Altruism: A Mixed-Methods Online RCT," *Applied Psychology: Health and Well-Being* 8, no. 3 (November 2016): 322–50, https://doi .org/1O.111/APHW.12074.

138 **The more hours over a lifetime:** See chapter 6 in Daniel Goleman and Richard Davidson, *Altered Traits: Science Reveals How Meditation Changes Your Mind, Brain, and Body* (New York: Avery, 2018).

Chapter 7

158 **Recently, with my old friend neuroscientist Richard Davidson:** Daniel Goleman and Richard Davidson, *Altered Traits: Science Reveals How Meditation Changes Your Mind, Brain, and Body* (New York: Avery, 2018).

160 **Another benefit of meditation:** Clifford Saron, presentation at second International Conference on Contemplative Science, San Diego, November 2016.

161 **For instance, seasoned *vipassana*, or insight, meditators:** Melissa A. Rosenkrantz et al., "Reduced Stress and Inflammatory Responsiveness in Experienced Meditators Compared to a Matched Healthy Control Group," *Psychoneuroimmunology* 68 (2016): 299–312.

163 **Several other studies:** J. D. Creswell et al., "Mindfulness-Based Stress Reduction Training Reduces Loneliness and Pro-Inflammatory Gene Expression in Older Adults: A Small Randomized Controlled Trial," *Brain, Behavior, and Immunity* 26, no. 7 (October 2012): 1095–101.

Chapter 8

182 **When Richard Davidson and I:** Our review of scientific findings on meditation is in Daniel Goleman and Richard Davidson, *Altered Traits: Science Reveals How Meditation Changes Your Mind, Brain, and Body* (New York: Avery, 2018), ch. 8.

183 **Indeed, one of the maxims:** For a fuller exploration of mindfulness and cognitive therapy, see Tara Bennett-Goleman, *Emotional Alchemy: How the Mind Can Heal the Heart* (New York: Harmony Books, 2001). See also A. B. Nejad et al., "Self-Referential Processing, Rumination, and Cortical Midline Structures in Major Depression," *Frontiers in Human Neuroscience* 7, no. 666 (October 10, 2013): https://doi.org/10.3389/fnhum.2013.00666.

184 **How our childhood attachments:** See, e.g., Jude Cassiday and Phillip Shaver, eds., *Handbook of Attachment Theory: Research and Clinical Applications* (New York: Guilford, 1999).

184 **The negative side:** James T. Tedeschi, *Impression Management Theory in Social Psychological Research* (New York: Academic Press, 2013).

185 **But long-term meditators:** Judson Brewer et al., "Meditation Experience Is Associated with Differences in Default Mode Network Activity and Connectivity," *Proceedings of the National Academy of Sciences 108, no. 50 (2011): 1–6, https://doi.org/10.1073 /pnas.1112029108.*

186 **Cognitive science has determined:** Cortland J. Dahl, Antonie Lutz, and Richard J. Davidson, "Reconstructing and Deconstructing the Self: Cognitive Mechanisms in Meditation Practice," *Trends in Cognitive Sciences* 19, no. 9 (September 2015): 515–23.

186 **Psychology, for example:** Chloe C. Banker and Mark R. Leary, "Hypo-Egoic Nonentitlement as a Feature of Humility," *Personality and Social Psychology Bulletin* 46, no. 5 (May 2020): 738–53, https://doi.org/10.1177/014616721987514.

187 **The science goes a step further:** Ruben E. Laukkonen and Heleen A. Slagter, "From Many to (N)one: Meditation and the Plasticity of the Predictive Mind," *Neuroscience & Biobehavioral Reviews* 128 (September 2021): 199–217, https://doi.org/10.1016 /j.neubiorev.2021.06.021.

INDEX